The power of Babel

Michel Pierssens

Professor of French at the University of Michigan

The power of Babel

A study of logophilia

translated by Carl R. Lovitt

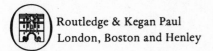 Routledge & Kegan Paul
London, Boston and Henley

This translation first published in 1980
by Routledge & Kegan Paul Ltd
39 Store Street, London WC1E 7DD,
Broadway House, Newtown Road,
Henley-on-Thames, Oxon RG9 1EN and
9 Park Street, Boston, Mass. 02108, USA
Set in IBM Journal by Hope Services, Abingdon
and printed in Great Britain by
Redwood Burn Ltd, Trowbridge & Esher
Translated from La tour de Babil
French edition © 1976 by Les Editions de Minuit
English translation © Routledge & Kegan Paul 1980

British Library Cataloguing in Publication Data

Pierssens, Michel

The power of Babel.
1. Languages — Philosophy
I. Title
401   P106.   79–42733
          .P47413
ISBN 0 7100 0373 0

Contents

The fiction of the sign

Logophilia

Before cross-breeding brought them together, unveiling a dramatic
epistemological reversal that keeps us fascinated by their fundamental
kinship, linguistics in the Saussurian tradition and psychoanalysis had
each elaborated a theory of language on their own. A double series
of representations had emerged: two 'sciences'. One considered the
specific manner in which the linguistic faculty invests itself in the
institution of the particular system of each language. The other sought
to discover how the signifying effects of each subject's desire are
inscribed, subterraneously, in his language. On the one hand, a system;
on the other, a speech. Language on the one hand; future *'lalangue'*[1]
on the other.

As in a play where two strangers are suddenly revealed to be brother
and sister, the dramatic Lacanian reversal immediately makes it possible
to understand that the rules of that same discourse, which the linguist
and the rhetorician presume to exhaust by confining its existence to
the registers of their order, are the very ones that the unconscious,
itself, 'speaks'.

The pathology of language, and specifically studies of aphasia, from
Jakobson to Luce Irigaray,[2] through Dubois and Hécaen, have already
taught us that linguistics and theories of certain psychotic disorders
can be successfully applied to one another.

Whether the unconscious be 'normal' or pathological, it is therefore
rooted and recoverable in the linguistic structure, whether it successfully
carries out its discourse or makes those mistakes by which it betrays
and thereby affirms itself. The subject will be located there, in that
scansion which distinguishes the statement from the utterance.

Yet in all these cases, language is not – or scarcely – reflected upon by those subjects who manifest through it the truth of their inherent split; for them, language remains largely in this realm of the practico-inert, a transparent opacity that must, in consideration of desire, be both maintained and worked through; this oxymoron is a necessity if there is to be *any* real. But there are other, more enigmatic cases where 'psychic disturbances' deprive language of its anonymity. On the contrary, for those who experience them, these disturbances of a different order seem to be inseparable from an intense attention to and an unappeasable curiosity for anything having to do with language. Here, language becomes more than just the scene of effects in the apparatus of the consciousness of unconscious conflicts; it is itself at stake.

Paranoiacs? Schizophrenics? Let us avoid hasty classifications that really teach us nothing. Out there is an entire nation of speech – alternately subjects and sovereigns or both at the same time – where great reformers of the science of language are too numerous to be counted, where we find untiring scriptors of regularly atypical *texts*, unconcerned with fashion, impervious to influences, adrift from the paradigms of an era through which they move, taking nothing but snatches of their discourses: an entire 'literature', a complete 'science' that eludes the rules of pure reason as much as the canons of the 'humanities', yet not without acknowledging both at times as their declared ambition, their secret regret. Nor can we exclude those writers who only briefly contributed to this strange '*enfer*'; the palimpsestic phantom of that 'other' discourse will always be found haunting everything they have written.

As much as the '*Art Brut*' that Dubuffet knew how to recognize,[3] these texts deserve to be examined because they solicit both our writing and our rationality: everything that constitutes for us the regime of 'signification' or that body of knowledge that stands as the guarantor of truth. Further, confronted with texts, *a* text, that can, indifferently, produce science or fiction from one another, the distinctions between 'science' and 'literature' are challenged and break down. These texts present an enigmatic knowledge that undoes our own, sets before it the impossible mirror of a non-knowledge that mimes it to the point of vertigo, in the questioning movement, unruled, unruly, of a single writing.

Among all those names that recur – without a 'discipline' ever emerging, and for good reason – in the contemporary discourse that treats the phenomena we are discussing (let us gather them, obliquely, under the inadequate rubric 'paragrammatism'), some are insistent: Lautréamont, Saussure, Roussel. Others cross the field, or are content to remain in the wings, 'off-stage' voices that hint at some vague kinship linked more by philosophical reflection than literary research: Brisset, Wolfson. Yet another mid-way between literature and philosophy: Mallarmé. But there would be room for still others: Desnos, Leiris, Ponge . . .

Yet what, beyond the shifting outline of an *'avant-garde'* relentlessly forging its own history, do these names indicate? Contemporary theories of language and writing have especially treated them as examples of a linguistic, social and historical *practice* capable of undoing codes, redistributing discourse, uprooting structures, subverting the illusions that blind our culture. These writers form the priceless heritage of an experimentation with language which a writing of the future could well address as a resource for answering its most pressing questions. And all share common properties that can be recognized even before the distinctions that will set linguists on one side, 'poets' on another, and 'madmen' on still another, are established.

Today, this recognition is being made by linguists; we are currently having explained for us what syntax, what signifying combinatory, what operations are produced to produce the *texts* that we are learning to read. And a linguistic preoccupation is no doubt especially marked in those texts whose quasi-scientific reflection is often quite developed, interspersed with fictions or mixed in with them. Yet, the theories of the *Mots anglais* are never treated in criticism except as a providential metalanguage for reading Mallarmé's poems, which an ivory tower conception of aesthetics thereby and forever maintains in isolation. Saussure's Anagrammes and the lectures that the *Cours de linguistique générale* distantly echo also remain separate in the epistemological gaze. Why? It is no doubt the expression of a will not to take their common ground, *fiction*, into account (Mallarmé: 'the eruption of dream into study').

For isn't it precisely this fiction that fascinates us as readers? Theoretical adventure novels that, for us, are also surface phenomena, that is events and itineraries where science refuses to see anything but the articulation of concepts in depth. Inseparable, fiction and 'science' animate all these writings – a primary fusion in a grey area where we perhaps fail to recognize *as well* the work of *passion*: enthusiasm and suffering. What is the status of Saussure's desire? That is the question.

The possibility that, through the incandescence of a single desire that possesses us, fiction may be the sister of science, is what requires our attention, to teach us that, behind the mirror of discourse, even forming its tain, there are *subjects*, speeches more or less bound up in the words.

Rather than reduce these experiences to a single logic, however complex (which we might perhaps reconsider later), should we not best begin by listening to these voices, networks of traces more or less embossed by a desire that may obey more than one law yet still retain order? We must heed the voice that dictates verse to Roussel, pronounces 'the penultimate is dead' to Mallarmé, blends the blast of trumpets at the Apocalypse to the voice of Brisset, martyrizes Wolfson's ears and corrodes his body by speaking English and inexhaustibly whispers anagrams to Saussure.

All have made the 'journey', but each time in a new and unexpected way, in an uncharted world. Those who don't disappear in it bring back irreducible lessons, *texts* whose implications are not exhausted by a study of their poetics (as Lebensztejn and Todorov have done[4]). Rather than concentrate upon cataloging the morphological mechanisms of their language, we should instead construct a model of a perhaps common *experience* that, from something resembling psychosis, gives birth to *logophilia* (to be provisionally yet cautiously distinguished from the 'semiosophia' of the eighteenth century: Meschonnic's word[5]). Our investigation must go beyond a fascination with curios, beyond the none the less positivistic satisfaction of having successfully identified a linguistic order in the débâcle of representations. Examining adventures that so profoundly and vigorously call into question the established (or to-be-established) order of language and the episteme, we find that the very situation of language between literature and desire is what comes to haunt our convictions. The contours of 'literature' (and of writing as well) become blurred, less simply suscep-tible to a strict linguistics or a decoding derived from a demystified psychoanalysis. And linguistics as a 'science' comes to reveal strange affinities with the things which its existence depends upon excluding.

Idumaea

Rediscovering the great play of language in a
single space could just as well be a decisive leap
towards an entirely new form of thought as a way of
closing back upon itself a mode of thought constituted
in the preceding century.

Michel Foucault

Let us go further. Open? Reseal? The entire problematics of our age
seem expressed in the aporia ticking with the uncertainty about what
makes time. Close, crack open, crease or unfurl the veil: problematics
of the look and of language, that yields a glimpse then steals away and
points to a forbidden realm beyond itself. Jameson refers to the
'Prison-House of Language'.[6] Each step brings us up against what
marks the performance of writing, the theater of concepts, the bleeding
of desire; in short, everything that is *ballet* for Mallarmé, once music – a
form of writing – has repressed the voice it no longer dares to hear.

The network of the signifier is the net in which we are snared by
the lure: 'glow beyond closure' (Derrida), the casement that provides
an opening on the constellations. We are that prisoner whose dream
makes Freud dream,[7] whereas in our sleep, eyes half-shut on the
dogmatisms haunting our cave, we see a procession of signifiers rise
up like a new Jacob's ladder that we will scale without end, knowing
there is nothing beyond except the impossible. But Brisset didn't know
that and, as a result, failed to return from the world sheltered by
the mirror.

Like Mallarmé, we no longer see our reflection in this mirror, but
in its place find 'Anguish': 'She, deceased nude in the mirror, and yet,/
In the oblivion closed off by the frame is fixed/Of scintillations
forthwith the septet.'[8]

Since Mallarmé, language and universe are always to be read in the
same words, and one in the other: mystery of mysteries framed by
'letters' – adventure of the 'madman' losing himself in the incessant
throw of the dice where his wandering trajectory is gradually undone;
adventure of the linguist eager to deny chance; adventure of the poet
who, on the contrary, welcomes it, to be in turn disseminated in it or
to triumph over it, 'word by word', inciting *fiction*.

These are three trajectories whose paths bifurcated near the turn
of the century, only to perhaps converge again today, designating,

revealing the obscure hearth, the unique Idumaea, that made them possible. These are all texts whose writing is an 'infinitization': pointing to that which lies beyond us, in writing, madness or science. This convergence can be understood from the fact that our science of language is henceforth a science-fiction. Once again we hear the clamour of the gods (Lacan[9]); once again (Kristeva, Sollers) we witness the vertigo of a madness that has stirred the text ever since the Idumaean chora[10]; once again signifying can be thought of in terms of the 'galaxy', the 'constellation'.[11]

Whence come the figures of a desire so present, though buried, and so general that all recognize themselves in it? What is this discourse that disarticulates the orders that enabled us to speak of madmen, scientists, poets – where all texts and all models (increasingly 'physical', according to Michel Serres' wish[12]) could be reinscribed? 'Paragrammatism' emerges throughout discourse and speech, creating a single space that, at times, implodes, at others, unfurls. It has even become – almost – a *genre*, and yet disrupts all genres. To it we owe the eradication of a conventional punctuation of time: from Cratylus to Virgil, from Court de Gébelin to Mallarmé, from Saussure to Roussel, from Wolfson to Sollers, an eternal present of the *sign* is invented, forever borne by languages, forever suffering, arrested by metaphysics and the histories that bind them, outlining orders soon undone that will have reassured for but an instant.

Could they all, in their 'madness', be the trace of a great crease in knowledge, the trauma of tottering horizons, that pause between two sciences when the second still eludes us while the first becomes progressively enigmatic? We must try to understand that chapter whose episodes bear the names of Mallarmé, Saussure and Brisset, yet which also encompasses such diverse figures as Schreber, Roussel, Wolfson . . . A 'history' in which psychosis, linguistics and fiction speak the same language and tell in their own dialect of the advent of a unique and varied adventure in the infinite space of the sign. *One* experience and *three* discourses.

'In truth, I journey, but in unknown lands . . .' (Mallarmé[13]). As a practice and as a theory, paragrammatism is the dream of a knowledge and of a freedom, of a liberation of the letter through an adherence to its network and journeys: promise of a thrill, certainty of 'glory' (Roussel, Brisset) for the castaways of the alphabet.

Our discussion of some of these adventurers cannot settle for those somewhat scornful 'biographèmes' that have served only to ignore their lives, especially not if the signs of life form the field of desire, if the resulting signs provide both the configuration of the various 'epochs of speech' (Court de Gébelin[14]) and the outline of that solitary space in which desire and sign, sign of desire and desire for the sign merge. These writings are a 'thanatography' in which the full figurative visibility of the 'biography' recedes into obscurity, as it does with Poe, where the gloomy slope of death speaks from behind the mirror (Mallarmé: 'Fortunately, I am perfectly dead'[15]).

Literature, madness, linguistics: three deliria born of the sign and desire. We will have to understand its logic and try to discover why the same experience which the eighteenth century made into a science was treated as madness in the nineteenth (Brisset and Saussure's century), while ours perceives a *writing* that permits everything to be thought anew, like before Babel, and perhaps to restart the cycle of a return that lays, spiral upon spiral, the discourses it will belie.

What is it, along this course, that distinguishes Mallarmé, Saussure and Brisset from one another? The first, back from Idumaea thanks to the therapeutic (N.B.: *similia similibus*) effects of his linguistic studies ('my refuge if need be'[16]), reverts to literature: 'I become once more a pure and simple writer of literature',[17] the petty bourgeois disdained by Breton. The second, following the plunge into anagrams, will renounce everything (but it is the cunning of reason), and make science his own sanctuary. The third, perhaps bolder, will make the journey to the end, and never more cast anchor in our world: his drift will have crossed science, history, languages, politics, religions . . . Pure apotheosis in the skies of Speech.

These are three separate courses marked by texts that nevertheless bear witness to a single experience in which each chooses to recognize or forget the truth he has more or less glimpsed – the whole revolving around *fiction*, lived or not. Each has experienced 'chance' as Bataille understood it, albeit contemplated from the bank regained by Mallarmé, repressed by Saussure, assimilated as history by Brisset who becomes its herald. Others – Roussel, Wolfson – will confirm how it can be lived, through 'novels' or 'psychosis'.

1 Mallarmé's madness*

*You think I'm mad? Someday I'll explain to
you that my madness lies elsewhere.*

Mallarmé to H. Cazalis, 1864

Mallarmé inaugurates: the first place is rightly his, as emblem of the
epoch that he opens, when *madness, science* and *fiction* combine to
form a new network in which henceforth the entire experience of
language will be inscribed. Since Mallarmé, this network weaves our
horizon, and charts the pathway of every adventure – whether one
attempts to escape it by aiming for that which is beyond signs or
Nothingness, or loses oneself in the infinity of those signs. Mallarmé's
trajectory is inscribed in this alternative; unlike others (Roussel, Saussure,
Brisset), his correspondence permits our following it in a certain detail.

To begin with, it is startling to note a peculiar consensus among
critics: for most, the winters in Tournon are never more than somewhat
erratic rediscoveries, by a self-taught Mallarmé, of the familiar chapters
of philosophy (or should we say, after Lacan, 'flousophie'); Being, the
Absolute, Nothingness, such as Mallarmé evokes them, immediately
translate into Hegel, Schopenhauer, the Kabbala, etc. This was such a
reassuring festival of the concept that we can only regret Mallarmé's not
having explored it with more order. This was a 'savage' philosophy, all
the more disconcerting because his library contains no trace of the
philosophers who appear to have touched him. Fortunately, there was
Villiers de l'Isle-Adam, the initiator.

And if this was not enough to legitimate our metaphysical knowledge,
one could always change registers, and allow our literary knowledge
to shed light on the obscurities of philosophy: after all, Mallarmé's
writing does nothing but fulfil – in a manner which, though extremist,
is orthodox even in its excesses – a pre-assigned niche in a tradition that
has accommodated countless others. How could one presume to be a
poet in the 1860s, especially after having so greatly admired Baudelaire,
without the reassuring seal of Powerlessness, Melancholy, Mania, etc. to

1

countersign and authenticate a poetics which remains after all quite obscure.

In one way or another, our rationality manages to secure a foothold. The emergence of a new knowledge – psychiatry, for example – may yield a new interpretation, but the procedure remains identical. Jean Fretet diagnoses: 'The example of Mallarmé reveals the association of a schizoid base with alternating moments of mild excitation and deep depression. The sterilizing inhibitions of the melancholic are supplemented by the haughty abstractions of the schizoid. Their conjunction gives rise to Mallarméan Nothingness.'[1]

All is said and everything is explained. Whether we are dealing with metaphysical crises or psychotic symptoms, causality remains intact. There surely are metaphysics *and* psychic disorders, a 'madness' in the experience of Mallarmé: he says so himself; but what we must do is follow their intertwined paths, explore their network, in order to make of this life and of this absence of work something other than an imaginary entity, something other than a series of disconnected stages. For this is what has been done. At times Mallarmé is everywhere – but *which* Mallarmé? The one at Tournon? The one of *Hérodiade*? The one of *Coup de dés*, of the *Mots anglais*, of *La Dernière Mode*? He divides periodically, ranging from the melancholic at Tournon, the delicate dandy of *La Dernière Mode*, the mercenary pedagogue of the *Mots anglais*, to the misunderstood prophet of the *Coup de dés*.

Are these not most likely tentative climbs along a single journey, anamorphoses of a *subject* nearly destroyed, like a few others, by an exceptional experience, who spent his life reassembling himself – at times withdrawing behind pretexts and alibis, at others returning to the dangerous slopes? The text of this life must be re-examined in its rough drafts and vellum bindings, in its ellipses and deletions. And, in so doing, avoid distinguishing *two* Mallarmés as two Saussures are distinguished.

The tradition for this type of interpretation is none the less established early: nearly all of Mallarmé's friends insist upon seeing his linguistic studies as a distraction, a change of pace which would relieve him from avid and exhausting investigations of the Ideal and the Absolute. Yet they fail to realize that this type of encouragement actually pushes him towards a confrontation with the truth – albeit defused – of his 'madness': *Hérodiade, Igitur, les Mots anglais*, 'hysteria', the 'glottic spasm' that killed him – so many intersections and nodes in a background of nothingness. Mallarmé passes from one to the other, intertwining their series, and returns only, with the help of science (like Saussure, but more abruptly – perhaps because he went further), to a bank that he senses drifting away. Science represented the promise of a mastery over that which deprived him of himself.

Thus the extreme rarefaction of the winters at Tournon, fled and overcome but always revived, accompanies him in silence, at the heart of his seldom-broken silence, and will only become manifest years later in the nearly indecent sprouting of those texts – *Mots anglais, Crayonné au théâtre, Variations sur un sujet* – which revolve around the *sign*. *Hérodiade* which he never stopped writing – almost the last word of his 'testament' – is actually Mallarmé before the Sign: the lamb sacrificed to spare the sacrificer. Similarly, Brisset, as will be shown later, remains in Idumaea; being the spokesman for the Word, he consents to disappear within it.

If there is to be a starting point for a reading of Mallarmé, one must surely begin with what he wrote to Aubanel, one day in 1866:[2]

> I simply wanted to tell you that I had cast the outline
> for my entire work, after having found the key to myself,
> cornerstone, or centre if you like, to avoid mixing
> metaphors – centre of myself, where I rest like a sacred
> spider on the principal threads emanating from my spirit,
> at the *intersections* of which I will weave the marvellous
> lace that I intuit, and which already exists in the bosom
> of beauty.

This is a peculiar way to avoid 'mixing metaphors': here is a 'centre' that is a network, a weave, the origin of which is both everywhere and nowhere ('centre of myself'), that exists only in the infinite decentring of the centre, in the manifold, identical yet different, reduplications of the intersections. 'Marvellous lace', projected beyond the self, yet designed to bring him back to himself.

Given the ineluctability of his experience, Mallarmé, here, both anticipates and sums up his entire life. Being dead, as he will affirm, he knows the pathway beforehand, and what it consists of, because he holds the *key* – the one 'that provides the joy of contemplating eternity and delighting in it, alive, within oneself'.[3]

This motif of the *key* is found in, and put to precisely the same use by, Saussure, Brisset, Roussel and Wolfson, but it is Mallarmé who causes its miracle to shine with the most brilliance:[4]

> Every man has a Secret within him, many die without having
> found it, and they will never find it, because dead, neither

3

they, nor it, will any longer exist. I am dead and resurrected
with the gem-stone key to my final spiritual casket. It is
now up to me to open it, in the absence of any borrowed
impression, and its mystery will emanate in an extremely
lovely sky.

For Saussure, it is the Secret of the anagram; for Brisset, the Word; for
Roussel, fiction; and for Mallarmé – Beauty. 'Emanation', with its
mystical connotations (this will never go much further in that direction),
is already the constellation of the *Coup de dés* or the 'septuor' of the
sonnet in 'yx'. Mallarmé is disseminated in a still, secular Eternity,
where everything occurs at once on the spread page of Time. On the
basis of this future anterior (which is also a Baudelairean 'sky' 'where
beauty blooms'), diachrony is deployed. In 1871, on the verge of
reaching Paris, Mallarmé re-examines what he had anticipated years
earlier, and discovers that it remains true:[5]

Like a man who thinks of leaving, I gather from furniture and
the diverse perspectives of a former promenade, those impressions possibly lingering there. Then, I interrupt my drama to
review in the fleeting depths the body of my works patiently
assembled during these four years, in order to come close to
actually completing it, for the rest of my days. This procedure
in itself, new in literature, seduces me: but certain escapes
from the perfected labour still fill me with delight, if I must
see them again, fixing them.

'Procedure' will be Roussel's word, and we shall re-encounter it.
'Labour' will always be Mallarmé's word for his 'linguistic studies',
whether he refers to them in his correspondence or in his *Autobiographie*.
Knowing the profound ties linking these studies to his experience, his
Work, he continues here to associate 'delight' with their memory.
Later, that will be forgotten. It is clear that, at this point, Mallarmé –
just as he redistributed his body and spirit according to the order of the
sciences (here it is I who anticipate) – can reconsider the experience which
'disseminated' him, and understand that these flashes – whether they
touch on the contemplation of Nothingness, the assumption of Beauty,
the terror of the Word or the secrets of linguistics – are all part of the
same, solitary thread.

The multiple unity of his adventure, of his exaltations and of his
deadlocks at last became perceptible – and perhaps even indifferent –
to him. Since he is 'dead', 'escapes' alone furtively revive his 'delight';
in Paris, with the exception of the nocturnal phantom of the Book, he

will find nothing but Fans, set rhymes, Toasts and Tombs.

But how did Mallarmé come to settle, as a 'sacred spider', at the centre
of his own being? *A priori*, everything begins simply with turn-of-the-
century neurosis. For four years, his correspondence attests to its
effects: 'peculiar sterility';[6] 'crushing powerlessness';[7] 'I am *sick in the
head*';[8] 'real debasement';[9] 'spleen';[10] 'worn out by unfortunate and
sterile work';[11] 'Doctor Bechet . . . told me that I had a nervous disorder';[12] 'I experience complete exhaustion';[13] 'a season of illness
which, attacking the "saint of saints", the very brain . . .';[14] 'sterile
despair';[15] 'I have almost lost my reason';[16] 'glimpsed instants border-
ing on madness';[17] 'hysterical crisis';[18] 'cataleptic absence';[19] 'disorder',
'total nullity';[20] 'a supreme winter of anxiety and conflict.'[21]

Let us concede that if we are dealing here with a mystical experience,
it certainly prolonged itself unduly, and that if, instead, Hegel and
Metaphysics are to blame, to them is being attributed an awesome re-
sponsibility! But let us not settle for rejecting these manifestly inadequate
interpretations, in order to replace them with a scarcely more satis-
fying psychiatric diagnosis. The 'malady' must still be allowed to speak,
in order to learn of its effects and of the conditions of these attacks.

A loss of *self* is the first effect upon which Mallarmé insists. More
precisely, a loss of the *image* of the self. The ordeal of the mirror
frequently intervenes during these difficult years, and always to authenticate the return of this lost image. By looking at himself, by being
able to see himself once again, Mallarmé *learns* that he has lost sight
of himself, and that, in the interim, some part of himself has left him.
The return of his own image signals a loss – that of the dream, which
could never represent itself on this side of the mirror:

> Me, I drag along like an old man and spend hours observing
> in mirrors the invasion of dumbness that dulls my droopy-
> lashed eyes and lets fall my lips;[22] Yes, I observe myself
> with horror, like a ruin;[23] seeing my degraded and lustre-
> less face, I draw back from mirrors, and weep when I feel
> hollow;[24] I fell, victorious, hopelessly and infinitely –
> until I finally saw myself again one day before my Vene-
> tian mirror, such as I had forgotten myself several months
> before.[25]

From this image that is no longer him or no longer only him, it takes
Mallarmé a period of time to outline the contour of something that he

5

had not yet seen. The destruction of his own image gives birth to the image that has taken its place, and which he cannot bring back in order to become himself again:

> [without a mirror] I would become Nothing again. This is to inform you that I am now impersonal and no longer the Stéphane you have known – but an aptitude which the spiritual Universe has of seeing and developing itself, through that which flees me;[26] The mirror which has reflected Being for me has most often been Horror.[27]

What the mirror reflects is no longer simply an image, but an inhabited depth, a pool, that is ordinarily not seen:

> the pool of the dream wherein we fish for nothing but our own image, without thinking of the silver scales of the fish;[28] an ancient dream had installed something like a marine grotto in me where it performed peculiar pieces, if I'm not mistaken.[29]

The *self* has disappeared in these waters: an exploded self, in tatters, effaced before the spectacles which inhabit it:

> There are great gaps in my brain which has long been incapable of sustained thought;[30] my brain, disintegrated and drowned in a watery twilight, has long forbidden me art;[31] I am veritably decomposed;[32] My thought has gone so far as to think itself and no longer has the strength to evoke in a unique Nothingness the void disseminated in its porosity;[33] My thought beginning to disseminate itself, I slip into my malaise.[34]

Mallarmé's ordeal of the mirror thus upends the constructive stage which Lacan contends it permits: through it, his body left its berth, fragmented. The self which it should have confirmed, instead, collapsed, revealing, where it vanished, nameless spectacles, which every name for the *void*, in turn, attempts to approximate without ever grasping. The experience is of the body and of the self – both undone.

But this does not exhaust the effects of the malady. If it attacks the self and the body, it affects, at the same time, that which joins and holds them together: *language*. In the débâcle, images alone do not plunge to the depths, the 'watery twilight' of 'the pool of the dream'. Speech *and* writing are both affected:

I swear to you that there is not a single word which has not cost me several hours of research;[35] I weep when I feel empty and am unable to cast a word on my implacably white paper;[36] when, after a day of waiting and of thirst, comes the holy hour of Jacob, the struggle with the Ideal, I haven't the strength to align two words;[37] And you could never believe how badly I speak, in flashes, without continuity, unable to complete my thought;[38] in the minutes of respite, I flung myself like a desperate maniac upon the elusive opening of the poem that sings in me, but that I cannot note;[39] hysteria threatened to disturb my speech;[40] the apparatus of language which my nervous disorder seems most intent upon disrupting,[41] an ailment which almost prevented me from reading and writing.[42]

And finally let us not overlook the celebrated glottic spasm which, in depriving Mallarmé of speech, kills him – closing scene in the drama of 'hysteria'. If Mallarmé discovered that he was centre and canvas, text and nothingness, it was through the experience of that negative miracle of dispossession and destruction which affects everything, from the body and thought to writing – and in the process reveals their mysterious unity. For if Mallarmé allows himself to be invaded by the otherness of multiplicity, it is also because he has sought it.

In depriving him of speech and paralysing his hand, this ailment does nothing, after all, but take hold of the instruments which gave rise to it. The 'powerlessness', destined to disrupt all his poetry and his entire poetics, itself originates in that poetry, and in the very gesture of writing:

having attained the horrible vision of a pure work, I nearly lost my reason and the meaning of the most familiar phrases;[43] I experienced disturbing symptoms caused just by the act of writing;[44] Unfortunately, by dredging the verse to such a point, I encountered two abysses, which cause me to despair: one is Nothingness, which I reached without knowledge of Buddhism, and I am still too disconsolate to believe even in my poetry and to resume the work which this crushing thought forced me to abandon;[45] my dream which, having destroyed me, will rebuild me.[46]

The self, language and poetry are engulfed in a common destruction, and founder in the same shipwreck – 'madness', which we can no longer pinpoint as the cause or the enigmatic product. The circularity

of the disasters deprives us of landmarks, and the play of reflections
henceforth occurs between mirrors that uproot the real ('what I lack
is reality'[47]). The poem can no longer be the fruit of serene plenitude:[48]

> I created my work through *elimination* alone; each acquired
> truth arose strictly from the loss of an impression which had
> glittered and then consumed itself, releasing shadows that
> guided me to the depths of the sensation of absolute Dark-
> ness. Destruction was my Beatrice.

The reign of visibility that should have been upheld by the images
in the mirror has given way to an obscurity that is only reached by
isolated sparks, whereas an invisible thread of forgotten horror, held
taut by 'evil', winds through the invisibility:[49]

> all of this has not been found through the normal develop-
> ment of my faculties, but through the sinful and hasty,
> satanic and *facile* path of the Destruction of myself, which
> produced not strength but a sensitivity which, fatally, led
> me there.

The familiar architecture which allows the body, language and reality
to exist together (a network inscribed in those of the real, the imaginary
and the symbolic orders) has crumbled. There can be no more centre,
and 'thought' has been randomly scattered by language scuttled, re-
conquered, erupted – a pulverized process of signification, that shimmers.
Mallarmé's seemingly whimsical claim that he would 'easily [place] the
larynx in the brain'[50] must be taken seriously. The strange coalescence
of these two symbols of speech and of thought manifests what has been
swept away by the eddy. The displacement to which Mallarmé subjects
them cannot be ascribed to simple word play; this shorthand reveals
instead, with illuminating depth, the nature of this 'malady': a drama
of language and of thought, of the signifier and of signification. Shortly
thereafter, seeking the framework that will allow him to restore 'larynx'
and 'brain' to their proper places, Mallarmé will endeavour to forget
the unbearable knowledge of terror and delight revealed to him by
writing.

It is his own body that will have to be recognized with the indifferent
and neutral grid of scientific discourse – a phantasmatic body, like
those of Bellmer's figures whose anatomies betray the dictates of
desires and suffering.

This phantasmatic investment of speech is also to be found in the discovery of that second 'abyss' which Mallarmé claims to have encountered while 'dredging the verse' (and let us also note that this word 'dredge' itself reinforces the fantasy of hollowing and even of evisceration: Nothingness and 'powerlessness'): 'the other void that I found is that of the chest.'[51] The physician whom he consults may well tell him that his ailment is not there ('He told me that I had trouble with my nerves, but that my chest was not affected'[52]), but he none the less persists in this belief: 'Above all, one must, through a life of exceptional care, prevent the débâcle – which will begin with the chest, infallibly.'[53] It is not indifferent that, as of 1864, he attributed his illness to the 'priapism of his youth',[54] stressing thereby the sexual symbolism of those attacks of powerlessness, sexualizing discourse and writing. Hérodiade is spawned in the throes of these attacks, whereas each period of remission is marked by a resumption of work on the Faune; the nights of darkness and diamonds oppose the afternoons of resurrection. Up to the glottic spasm, nothing serves perhaps so well as the ultimate precipitate of this network of beliefs (the glottis is a phallic substitute), in accomplishing the fatality which they foresaw.

But if the chest is empty, it is on account of speech; and it is through speech, blending these empty words, that the *self* may, perhaps, sustain its life. This 'malady must be accepted as permanent; it must be counted upon; one must acquire an experience and a habit which may, at least, thwart its effects'.[55] Announcing *Igitur* to Cazalis, Mallarmé regains strength with the help of this homeopathic belief:[56]

> it is a tale with which I want to crush the old monster of Powerlessness, its subject at least, in order to cloister myself in my great labour which I have already restudied. If it is done (the tale), I am cured; *similia similibus*.

The void must be treated with the void; the dispersion and the débâcle, with poetry – 'chance vanquished, word by word'. It is enough to say that everything circulates through the net of words: a Nothingness which is nothing but an image of the *self*, an Idea which is but the void of things. The poem will have nothing more to say than that – too bad for the meaning. Mallarmé admitted this to Cazalis, summarizing at once all the figures we have seen him trace; it is when he describes a possible illustration for one of his sonnets:[57]

it seems to lend itself to an etching filled with Dream and Void.

   For instance, an open, nocturnal window, with both shutters latched; a room without occupants, despite the stable air presented by the latched shutters, and in a night made up of absence and interrogation, without furniture, if not the plausible sketch of vague consoles, a bellicose and agonizing frame, of a mirror hanging in the rear, with its stellar and incomprehensible reflection of the great Bear, which links to the sky alone this dwelling abandoned by the world.

The 'septuor' of the sonnet in 'yx' is a mirror where 'Anguish' is inscribed in a stellar fashion and upon which this now disunited *self* will be projected; his only existence will be in the sowing of the words, with which he will form a constellation:[58]

   I take this sonnet, which I had thought of once this summer, from a projected study on *Speech*: it is inverted; namely, its meaning, if it has one (but I would be consoled by the contrary owing, so it seems, to the dosage of poetry it contains), is evoked by a mirage of the words themselves.

   Mirror, speech, obliterated meaning, stellar portrait of a face erased: the poem will be all of these, as its scope will be limited to the relations between the words. Thus the Nothingness, wherein the words are articulated, may be contemplated from the other side of the mirror, deprived of its threat of death and madness. Henceforth, a poetics is assured:[59]

   Chance does not initiate a verse, that is the great thing. We have, several of us, attained that, and I believe that, with lines so perfectly delineated, what we must especially aim for, in the poem, are words – which are already enough themselves not to receive impressions from without – that so reflect each other as to lose their own colour, and become but transitions along a scale.

   This marks the end of reflections in the mirror; in fleeing the darkness of 'Being', all light flows toward and seeks refuge in the words: 'virtual trail of fire across gems'. This is the 'Secret', the 'gem-stone key to my final spiritual casket'. Yet this key, and the gems and jewels adorning it, have another name; for all of Mallarmé's life they summa-

rized what Mallarmé took back from the mirror in order to master its
'Ideal' and its 'Nothingness'. This key is a name: Hérodiade. Within
it lies all language, all poetry, every possibility for survival:[60]

> The loveliest page of my work will be the one that contains
> only that divine name *Hérodiade*. What little inspiration I
> have had I owe to this name, and I believe that, had my
> heroine been called Salomé, I would have invented this
> sombre word, red as an open pomegranate, Hérodiade.
> Furthermore, I wish to make her a being purely dreamed
> and absolutely independent of history.

This affirmation must also be taken seriously and *literally*, as it
states the link between the letter and desire, the abolition of meaning
and the abolition of time, and the very possibility of fiction. Given
Hérodiade's indifference to time, this would in fact signify an indifference to the accidents of life. In 1864 Mallarmé said of the text of
Hérodiade: 'I would never again touch a pen if I were crushed'[61] by
writing it. In fact, in a certain manner, he never again touched the pen
that the poem might have disappointed. Or rather, he was never again
able to set it down ¬ terror of the deadlock perhaps, and of a possible
return to Idumaea? For his entire life, Mallarmé will have been *in the
process of* writing his *Hérodiade*: 'work of my ravished nights',[62]
Hérodiade, 'where I had stripped naked without knowing it, whence
my doubts and malaise, and for which I finally found the last word.'[63]
This 'last word' is none other than the very name upheld by its reflecting syllables in its shimmering Nothingness; it condenses the entire
language and is the resource for the *self*. Mallarmé, henceforth an
'impersonal' figure, will never be more than language itself; only in
the trace of its play will he remain a subject.

Yet, in assuring itself of an eternity won from time, such a discovery
('spiritual conception of Nothingness'[64]) dances upon the ashes of
instants; it is made up entirely of that which destroys. In an astonishing
letter to Lefébure – the very letter, previously discussed, in which he
refers precisely to the fantasy of the 'empty chest' – he says: 'Each
birth is a destruction, and every life of a moment is the agony in
which we revive what we have lost, to see what we hadn't known before.'[65]

Here, going a bit further, we can penetrate the phantasmatic tissue
from which Hérodiade springs like a new-born child; the endometral
lace which nurtured it (Mallarmé speaks of the 'marvellous lace' of his

future poems) is ruined in its own destruction, and thereby permits the birth of the Dream. Hérodiade is born three times, in three simultaneous spaces: from Nothingness (on the 'spiritual' plane), from the empty chest signifying death (on the plane of 'Speech'), and from a destroyed womb (according to an imaginary conception of the body).

This marks the discovery of a feminization of the body through writing and language against which Mallarmé (like Président Schreber) rebelled. In order to avoid inhabiting the woman's body that subjects him to a painful pregnancy, he will struggle to reaffirm sexual differences (La Dernière Mode will be the afterbirth of this event, just as Schreber's disguises in the mirror were designed to prove that he was still the woman destined for God). Still in the same letter, Mallarmé in fact opposes woman's 'passive destruction' to man's active destruction (where we rediscover the idea that he is paying for the 'priapism of [his] youth'). To abuse her, he recalls the name given by woman to that which characterizes her as such (her period): her 'affaires'. This is the word used by 'imbecilic' men 'to satisfy social necessities': ' "J'ai mes affaires", both signifying two different things, yet basically identical. Were I to write a cantata, it would enter the Choir and be divided into masculine and feminine stanzas.'[66] Yet Mallarmé writes not a cantata but a canticle, St John's, in which the image of castration is clearly implied. Setting the sexes opposite one another, Mallarmé proceeds to blend them – precisely because he wants to be neither the one nor the other:[67]

> I have since told myself, in those hours of necessary synthesis, 'I am going to work from the heart,' and I feel my heart (my entire life no doubt bears upon it), and the rest of my body forgotten, save the hand which writes and this heart which lives, my outline proceeds – proceeds –

We surely touch here upon the most complex aspect of the Mallarméan drama. Mallarmé's own representations reveal the metamorphoses involved, as they cut across his body, his sex, his language. Hérodiade is all of this: bloody monster and scintillating dream, impenetrable body and word disclosing the infinite. 'I am veritably decomposed, and to say that it takes all that to have a view truly – one of the Universe! Otherwise, you feel no unity other than that of your life.'[68] Destruction and resurrection, death and life are summed up in the unity of the dream for which Mallarmé goes into labour and to which he gives birth, and this is Hérodiade; Igitur would be her double, her underside. Thus, for Mallarmé, Nothingness may be subdivided – light and life in Héro-diade, ash and darkness in Igitur.[69]

> On the ashes of the stars, the indivisible ones of the family,
> lay the poor character who had drunk the drop of nothing
> missing from the sea (the empty phial, folly, all that remains
> of the castle?) Nothingness departed, there remains the castle
> of purity.

Having drunk the phial (*fiole*): the signifier of his suicide and an ana-gram for his madness (*folie*), Mallarmé could say that he was 'dead'. And this suicide is his cure: 'If it is done (the tale), I am cured; *similia similibus.*'[70]

And then *desire* awakens. From his collapse, from his ashes, some-thing can be reborn; and the word, all words contained in one, all of language will exist only to give meaning to this new event. This is ad-mittedly a dream, but one in which Mallarmé underwent a total metamorphosis in order to be able to desire himself again. No fortuity whatsoever is to be found in these verses from *L'Après-midi d'un faune* (hinting at the longed-for vernal rebirth opposed by the wintry Héro-diade), which reinvoke the *pomegranate* which had first been the very name of Hérodiade:[71]

> You know, my passion, already ripe, that purple,
> Each pomegranate bursts and bees murmur;
> And our blood, with what will seize it, afire,
> Flows for the eternal swarm of desire.

The *self* has split forever; it is an image that is lost, then reincarnated in the now visible other, offered up to his desire. It is here that Mallarmé is closest to Brisset, Roussel, Saussure and Wolfson: words open, burst, and emit dancing, unstable, evanescent, and yet captive, forms, through which language – all languages – are grasped. Words form swarms which a mysterious Eros reassembles and destroys. Mallarmé's experience will yield poems; Saussure's, antique names; Roussel's, adventures and novels; Brisset's, empires; Wolfson's, a body to save. In the process, desire finds itself and escapes, tracing the course of what it alone has lost: history, image, body, narrative. Nothing can continue to exist –

that is represent the real for desire; it must dispose of words to dispense and recombine in sonorous elements, words that will distract those lights which the mirror can no longer form alone, and, thereby, produce the impossible image which will never have a reflexive existence.

But, no more than Saussure, and not far beyond Roussel, can Mallarmé sustain himself to the end of such an apotheosis: 'I spend moments close to madness glimpsed in equilibrating ecstasies', 'I am coming down from the absolute.'[72] How do you 'come down' without losing everything? How do you keep alive the phantom that the words had permitted you to glimpse for an instant? Like Saussure, like the entire epoch which sealed the encounter between the sign and desire in this unique manner – but according to different modalities, and with differing results – Mallarmé found an ally which preserved both the Dream and Reason: linguistics.

None the less, this outlet, discovered at the bottom of the phial drained of folly, does not disclose itself in an instant. 'Nothingness' may be a matter of enlightenment – but its flash gives way to a long and difficult journey. As was the case for Saussure and for all the others, a return to the profane universe requires protracted patience: a period henceforth marked by 'toil' applied to scholarly research. Mallarmé would take several years to cover this path. Having seen the light, he turned away at first, disseminated in the multiple fires of words, only to triumph when, from behind the mystery of the *tongue*, there emerged that of *language*.

It may be possible to grasp that mythic moment when everything begins, the moment at which madness and language are still united. For example, we may seek it in 'Le Démon de l'analogie', written in 1864 at Tournon, when the 'malady' developed. 'The Penultimate is dead' – 'obscure phrase', 'in a signifying void'. But it becomes all the more significant if something snaps when 'the *null* [pen*ul*timate] sound' detaches itself. The sentence is null; as is the 'voice'. A word divides, and another emerges from and designates its destruction at the moment at which the voice splits, its void becoming the only plenitude. This is the discovery of the underside of words which speaks, as it does for Saussure, Roussel, Brisset or Wolfson, in a void: sense taking form in nonsense.

Mallarmé tells us better than the others that the internal split which affects words and serializes signifiers is *the subject who recognizes himself for what he is*; after the 'Penultimate', the voice in effect marks a 'silence' 'in which', Mallarmé adds, 'I found a painful *delight*' (my

italics). Delight becomes possible with the assumption of death and castration – but it is accompanied by its ineluctable inverse: 'I advanced
murmuring with an intonation inviting condolence: "The Penultimate is
dead, it is dead, quite dead, the despairing Penultimate", believing thereby
to dispose of *anxiety* . . .' (my italics). But it is in vain: 'fright' returns
and even 'anguish', 'beneath which my deposed spirit agonizes'.

Nothing will suture the fractured word, which confronts the subject
with his own split and his castration. His life will be no more than a
'mourning'; its interminable 'work', which will take Mallarmé through
the experience of *Hérodiade* and *Igitur*, and convert these texts into an
attempt to liquidate and negate his mourning. But his hope of forget-
ting is perhaps better achieved through *science* – and not just any science.
As of this text Mallarmé outlines the movement of that science, 'alleg-
ing, to calm myself, that, clearly, penultimate is the term in the lexicon
signifying the next-to-last syllable of words, and its apparition, the
poorly abjured remnant of a linguistic labour through which my noble
faculty daily laments its interruption.'[73]

We witness here the formation of what will constitute the future
course of the Mallarméan experience: linguistics is in no sense a marginal pursuit, a concession, an encumbrance; it is reason's rampart
against the truth discovered in the shattering of words, which is mimed
by poetry. It is the culmination of all his resistance but it is also a *compromise* with the truth: that which sutures shall be braided with that
which must be obscured: the inverse and inferno of words, a burning
treasure of signifiers. Thirty years later, 'Hérodiade', that word of
ashes and blood, will have survived as no more than a 'sign' – '. . . she
gives you, through the veil that never falls, the nudity of your concepts
and silently will write your vision in the manner of a Sign, which she
is.'[74] In 1868 this was stated quite differently: 'I have commited the
sin of seeing the Dream in its ideal nudity, whereas I should have in-
stalled between it and myself a mystery of music and oblivion.'[75] Time
will have draped a 'veil' over that which was not to be seen, on pain of
madness – veil of language, braid of words. Linguistics alone will have
permitted this transparent screen to be erected.

Mallarmé's undertaking was initiated very early: as of 1866 he connected 'science' with a 'powerlessness' which struggled against it and
disrupted its claim to *delight*:[76]

> my clouded spirit resists every effort to restore its former
> lucidity, and I am sadly resigned, on a divan, amidst heaps

of books that I peruse and leaf through without the courage
to complete them. It is true that they are books of science
and of philosophy and that I want to *delight* . . . for myself
in each new notion and not learn it. (Mallarmé's italics)

In 1868, the sonnet in 'yx' is said to be 'extracted from a projected
study of *Speech*' and its problematic meaning is 'evoked by an internal
mirage of the words themselves.'[77] Mallarmé is therefore concerned
with devising a simultaneous recourse to *fiction* and to *science*. Mallarmé is singularly close to Brisset when he, too, designates 'the Word'
as that which contains the history of man within its folds – just as
Hérodiade, the word and the veiled figure, contains Mallarmé's within
her own. This is confirmed by the precious *Notes* of 1869 and
1895:[78]

Every method is a fiction, and is useful for demonstration.
It seemed to him that language was the instrument of fiction: he will follow the method of language (determine it).
Language reflecting itself. At last it occurs to him that fiction is the very process of the human spirit: it animates
every method and reduces man to its will.

Further, he adds:[79]

OF SCIENCE. – *Having found a confirmation of itself*
in Language, Science must now become a CONFIRMATION
of Language.

As of this moment, everything becomes simplified – beginning with
suffering and its consort, exaltation. Science reduces the one to the
other: 'Having relocated all my thought in the presence of a book, I became involved in (linguistic) studies, my refuge if need be.'[80] This gave
rise to the *Notes* of 1869, quoted above, and led, somewhat later, to the
Mots anglais. In fact, it is in the very letter in which he announces his
immersion in science that Mallarmé draws attention to the 'course' that
he is organizing in town. Yet, as he states in the *Mots anglais*, all his
knowledge derives from his teaching. Another letter, written several
months later, marks, with concision, the links which organize his diverse
adventures into a single network of events:[81]

To make but one effort for the whole ['my life, and health

and career'], I chose linguistic subjects, hoping furthermore, that this special effort would not fail to influence that entire apparatus of language which my nervous illness primarily seems to affect . . . alongside, I can glimpse the structure of the slowly-developing work of my heart and of my solitude: in fact the other, parallel labour is, of it as well, but the *scientific foundation*. (my italics)

Linguistics ('labour'), 'nervous illness', and poetry ('work of the heart') thus proceed from the same, single womb which engenders them in the same movement. Yet as the illness regresses, the 'work' becomes more difficult – whereas the 'labour' gains strength, and becomes an increasingly reliable means of preservation. The possibility of knowledge, even knowledge itself, is reconstructed around linguistics:[82]

Yet, my linguistic studies require certain notions which are sufficiently simple to be retained as such in memory. . . . Could you indicate for me two works, elementary yet precise, on Physics and on Chemistry . . . ; you would also indicate a *fine little* Anatomy, and also a *natural History*.

This takes us some distance from the *Hérésies artistiques* which condemned Science in the name of Art ('poetry will be degraded to the rank of a science'[83]). Mallarmé even envisions crowning his encyclopedic reconquest by 'occupying [himself], preliminarily, with mathematics . . . .'[84] Nevertheless, fifteen years later, even though his lustral immersion in scientific discourses may have shielded him from madness and his Dream, Mallarmé will have reverted to his earlier antipathy.

Having redefined his 'vice' (the desire to complete his 'Great Work', the 'Book' – 'with the patience of an alchemist'; 'Chemistry', no doubt too simple, having been discarded), Mallarmé disdainfully notes in the *Autobiographie* of 1885 composed at the request of Verlaine, what came of his salutary journey through science: 'In troubled moments or in order to buy harmful goods, I was compelled to perform certain neat tasks; none of this (*Dieux antiques, Mots anglais*) is worth speaking of.'[85] Henceforth, Science and Poetry ostensibly will have no knowledge of one another; their common origin is shrouded by their mutual silence. Poe's *Sonnet to Science*, which Mallarmé translated, alone retains a trace of this truth' 'Why should he [the poet] possibly care for you? Or would he adjudge you wise, you, who would prevent him, in his flight, from seeking a treasure in the jewelled sky, even if he had climbed there with an untamed wing.'[86] Reading the *Mots anglais* we will know henceforth what it was that spoke before it silenced him; but a distant rumble persisted in its echoes.

Returning for a moment to those conventional distinctions which – from a tendency to classify discourses without bothering to differentiate between the subjects of writing – enable us, for example, to treat Mallarmé and Lautréamont as *a priori* comparable writers, we find that an ambiguity must be dispelled. Doing so will enable us to understand the extent to which Mallarmé's experience is *unique*, and thus requires something other than the customary approach.

Contrary to the claims of a recent tradition, the Mallarmé/Lautréamont complex, conceived of as the pivot of an entire epoch, is nothing more than apparent. What do the two *experiences* of Mallarmé and Isidore Ducasse have in common? Schizophrenia could be cited. Yet neither Dr Soulier nor Dr Fretet has succeeded in convincing anyone: their only achievement is to have cast doubt upon the validity of their science.[87] Psychiatry, to the extent that it is even able to describe, is too quick to classify, and judges too hastily to adequately understand. *Writing* could be cited. But Philippe Sollers intrigued more than he convinced when he saw a kind of allegory for writing itself in the text of the *Chants de Maldoror*. The same could be said of Julia Kristeva's thesis (on this point, at least[88]), when she proposed Ducasse and Mallarmé as two great transformers of the mechanics of meaning, working in some parallel fashion.

Whereas the notion of a conflict between the 'semiotic' and the 'symbolic' may in fact be upheld on the basis of precise documents left behind by Mallarmé, making such a claim for Ducasse's texts is a more adventuresome task – particularly in the absence of an internal criticism of his texts, and a sufficiently nuanced study of the relations between the *Chants de Maldoror* and the *Poésies*. Nothing authorizes our extrapolating Mallarmé's experiences and applying them to Ducasse himself. With the exception of a few letters (which are, incidentally, extremely important and insufficiently analysed), Ducasse left nothing behind which marks his position as a literary and as an extra-literary *subject*. Nowhere is the absence of a *biography* more apparent than in those studies which have tried to fill that gap[89] – however detailed or precise they may be.

Preferring not to undertake a lengthy study, I would nevertheless like to mark, on the basis of a few simple observations, what it is that sets Ducasse at a considerable distance from Mallarmé, as well as from Saussure, Brisset, Wolfson and Roussel. This is not to say that the *effect* of Ducasse's texts is not comparable to the one produced by their texts: it is simply to stress that, as subjects, their *loci* appear to have very little in common.

Of them all, Ducasse is the most controlled, the most sovereign, the one least at the mercy of the forces of language. Ducasse's thesis mystified the Surrealists: it was rationalistic, logocentric and even moralizing; it would even seem to invert the relation between the 'semiotic' and the 'symbolic' which Julia Kristeva posited for Mallarmé. If one heeds the discursive strategy which organizes each 'stanza' of the *Chants* as an oblique apologia in which the 'voices' of 'Good' and 'Evil' are perfectly identifiable, this thesis can be discerned quite early, and will be found to assert itself more and more as the *Chants* progress. This thesis is codified in the *Poésies*. It could be summarized thus: having emulated the models instituted by the Romantics in order to utilize their crushing and morally disruptive power for a paradoxical rectification (in accordance with the theory and method of *excess*, which had been widely used in the two centuries preceding his writing), Ducasse came to the realization that writing does not set up a relation with an imaginary order which it would then express; writing, on the contrary, *generates* that order. It produces effects of representation and, most importantly, produces affects, according to a regulated logic whose process he undertakes to reveal.

For Ducasse, the text is a production of representations and affects, which is entirely subordinate to a syllogistic, and bound in a discursive field swept by 'maxims' that can only deceive if the moral premises of writing are 'false'. He envisions nothing other (he puts it partially into practice in the *Poésies* by 'correcting' certain texts) than to master this textual machine in order to produce 'good' representations, that is, those he adjudges sound. He undertakes this project in opposition to the moral degradation which he, like many of his contemporaries, attributes to Romantic literature. From this perspective, it is upon the texts and life-styles of Hugo, Musset, Dumas, etc. that the 'semiotic' imposes its prosody; Ducasse, on the other hand, wants to restore them to the exclusive control of the 'thetic'. This is the philosophy, the strategy, which underpins the *Chants* and the *Poésies*; only the tactic differs from one text to the other. It is just a question of the 'method'.

The success of such an undertaking strictly depends upon a semiotic theory and practice profoundly respectful of the implicit order governed

en it poses the signified as a transcendental agency. The
is not being challenged here. Ducasse is incontestably
nd even a Hjelmslevian; according to Ducasse, the
'figures' at the different levels of expression must, auto-
....y, *produce* similarly articulated contents. From what he calls
the 'first principles' through to the ultimate determination of the
henceforth innocuous sentence as *pharmakon*, the whole can only
guarantee the transitivity of the True and the Good.

For Ducasse, language thus remains tied, in a fairly classical sense,
to the representation that it produces – by making the affects, and
thus the fantasies thereby evoked, somewhat difficult to control (this
is the node of his thesis) – or that it analyses. Language is a *logic* that
must be made more rigorous; it is a calculation of the meaning that
would never dislocate the sign, seeing as it is only designed to reinforce
the subordination of the signifiers to the signifieds. The *Chants de
Maldoror* constitute negative proof: manoeuvres within the signifier
which show that, without meticulous care, language becomes muddled,
where the slightest metaphor becomes a frenetic novel, a Byronic poem,
or a vulgar detective story. Everything that Roussel delights in, that
enables Brisset to produce an unknown history like a magician from a
top hat, that permits Mallarmé to conjure up the memory of the Dream
in peace – all this, Ducasse suppresses. The rarefaction which he attains
in the *Poésies* does not allow for the 'expansion' or 'spaciousness'
found in Mallarmé; there is only a 'development' guaranteed by the
sign of logic. In reuniting grammar, logic, rhetoric, and morality,
Ducasse announces a return to Port Royal. Mallarmé, on the contrary,
opting for reverie and governed by the logic of his adventure, surrenders,
like Brisset, to the enchantments of eighteenth-century linguistics.

As stated, linguistics provides Mallarmé, in the strictest sense of the
word, with a *discipline*. It permits him to restore order to the *self*, and,
thereby, to differentiate between science, poetry, and madness – the
first two having formed an alliance to eradicate madness, extenuated
in a 'dream'. Henceforth the poem becomes fragmented, slackens,
blooms with undecideables, but *syntax* presides, providing 'a guarantee':
'A stammering, that seems the sentence, here repressed in the use of
incidental multiples, composes and removes itself to some superior
equilibrium, with the foreseen balancing of inversions.'[90]

But it is a simplification to refer here to '*a* linguistics'. For Mallarmé,
there are in fact *two* linguistics or perhaps two intermingled *beliefs*
about the nature of the sign: two types of knowledge, parallel yet woven

20

with anastomoses, developed gradually in the course of the adventure analysed above. This ambivalence, owing to a fascination with a withdrawn dream replaced by negation, situates their common origin in the experience of the split between *Igitur* and *Hérodiade*. The knowledge of the sign, summarized by the very name of Hérodiade, was supplanted by the poetics theorized in the *Mots anglais*. Yet, what was repressed of this knowledge returned to carve a double scene in the words, for which Mallarmé's linguistic 'science' provides, perhaps unwittingly, a simultaneous double notion.

Examining the *Mots anglais* permits a clearer perception of this effect. At that time, when philology reigned, one reference served to indicate 'modernity' and the seriousness of the theoretical paradigm adopted by Mallarmé; that reference was to Grimm and his Law:[91]

> From Latin and Greek, situated at about the same level, to all Teutonic idioms, search for what takes place (if something special happens); now, it is a permutation of consonants, letters having a rare importance (...). Such is the law of Grimm, named for its inventor, the most famous German grammarian.

Brisset would remain superbly unaware of this law – unless he censored it, so as to better affirm the law of his own desire. Saussure, after having inscribed his initial career in the epistemological space opened by this law and its derivatives, would proceed to discover another which was to usher in an entirely new modernity for which the temporal and formal relations between languages differ markedly from Grimm's. To achieve this, he would have to backtrack, in a sense, to rediscover the *sign* and to give it a new theoretical status.

None the less, something decisive and enduring did emerge from Grimm's science: the distinction between the *letter* and the *sound*: 'For the first time, with Rask, Grimm and Bopp, language (although there is no longer an attempt to reduce it to its primal cries) is treated as a group of phonetic elements.'[92]

But what then of Mallarmé's interpretation of Grimm's law, if, to implement it, he makes use of precisely what it should preclude? Clearly, what Mallarmé has done is to posit the equivalence of the *sound* ('the consonants') and the *letter*, whereas the latter should serve only to note the former (and yet this principle can lead to considerable ambiguities, and even to an entire history). It is true that Grimm himself commits such infractions of his own rule; as Michel

Foucault recalls, 'he analyses *Schrift* as eight elements, because he divides *f* into *p* and *b*.'[93]

Yet, what appears as an inconsistency in Grimm's work is a systematic practice in Mallarmé's. Beneath the cloak of philology, Mallarmé explores a completely different and resolutely archaic science. The entire theory of the *Mots anglais* is rooted in conceptions that were in fact those of the eighteenth century – conceptions which the nineteenth century had presumed to have annulled. This is made abundantly clear by another aspect of Mallarmé's linguistics which, furthermore, may help to explain the nature of the distortion to which he subjects the new science that he purports to follow. I am referring to the insistence with which he, relentlessly, returns to the question of the *very origin of meaning* – a question he continues to raise even though he persists in announcing it as insoluble. This problem will be examined at a later point, after having relocated it as a pause in the work of a few others. It suffices here to draw attention to a particular preoccupation of Mallarmé, which makes him a successor to the Cratylists of the eighteenth century, a disciple of de Piis, of de Bosses, of Court de Gébelin: the question of onomatopoeias:[94]

> So perfect a link between the signification and the form of
> a word that it seems to cause but one impression, that of
> its success, to the spirit and the ear, is frequent; but especially
> in what we call ONOMATOPOEIAS . . . They perpetuate
> in our dialects a procedure of creation that was perhaps the
> first of all.

Let us make note here of this word 'procedure' which we shall come upon again as a marker. Onomatopoeia thus becomes the model, the archetype for what may have been the primordial *womb*, the *seed* of all signification inscribed in a sign. 'Hérodiade' is just such an original success; no other signifier, 'Salomé' for example, would have the power to be its substitute. Therefore, onomatopoeia is not the illustration of some linguistic ideal; it is the actual foundation of both the method developed in the *Mots anglais*, and of any authentic poetry. It is clear, however, that beneath the convenience of taxonomy, the method of the book betrays the same desire as did the verse. This is confirmed by the 1895 *Notes*:[95]

> No juvenile simplification in fact could persuade me, owing

to ancient subtleties that slay us, yet extracting the metal from their chimera, that there does not exist, I refer back to the already quoted case [the *s* of the plural], and do so philosophically without reference to grammar, lest it be a latent and particular philosophy as well as the armature of language, a relationship, yes, mysterious, admittedly, between for example this *s* of the plural and the one added to the second person singular, of verbs, expressing, it, no less than the one caused by number an alteration . . . from the standpoint of the speaker . . . *S*, I say, is the analytical letter; pre-eminently dissolving and disseminating.

Such research on the 'pure general sign that must mark the verse' is rigorously identical to that which serves as a methodological rule for the orderly constitution of the 'nomenclature' proposed for the *Mots anglais*: 'Meaning, of course, and sound, skilfully paired, these are the two sign posts guiding the Philologist in familial classification.'[96]

Calling himself a Philologist here manifestly constitutes a deviation – even if one were to concede that Mallarmé had preliminarily extracted the 'metal' from 'the chimera' of 'ancient subtleties'. This amounts to negation: the entire Mallarméan phantasmatics is inscribed in this network of obscurities disguised as enlightenments. We need only note for example the word 'familial' used to qualify the 'classification'. Doesn't it occur here only because the paternal and phallic sound around which the family will regroup is already suffused with a purified meaning to be combined? – which is clearly not a property of a *letter* conceived of as a convenient alphabetic resource:[97]

now the English reader does nothing besides consider the letters, beneath which groups of words gather, like *patronymic* initials when there is . . . an attempt to explain the Signification of more than one word by the Dominant Consonant: this entails a gathering of notes, provided by observation, useful to a few efforts of Science, but not yet deriving from it. (my italics)

The concepts of phonetic empiricism and 'familialism' thus enable Mallarmé to affirm a distance between a method and a future science; but this is only a rhetorical precaution designed to conceal, beneath the respected emblem of 'observation', an extremely precise conception which is systematically practised throughout the book. Mallarmé actually refines his schema by specifying even further the localization of meaning and modalities of combination whereby it appears. In this regard, Mallarmé treats the signifier in much the same way as would Saussure, Brisset, and Roussel, but he does so in order to extract a completely different practice and knowledge:[98]

> The meaning that can result from various combinations, is, within the limits of exact observation, the sole object of the Notes accompanying this nomenclature, and yet it is only at the beginning of words that anything happens: but it is fitting to add that it is there, *in the assault*, that signification truly resides.

Though a tentative belief, the argument for the method actually possesses all the characteristics of a theory; and, despite what Mallarmé may say about it, there is no difference in going from the 'task' to the 'work'. Beyond any pedagogic alibi, concerning Poetry, he repeats:[99]

> Such a magisterial effort of the imagination desirous, not only of satisfying itself through the symbol bursting in the spectacles of the world, but also of establishing a link between these and the speech responsible for expressing them, touches upon one of the sacred or perilous mysteries of language; and it will only be prudent to analyse this the day when Science, possessing a vast repertory of all idioms ever spoken on earth, writes the history of the letters of the alphabet throughout the ages, and what was nearly their absolute signification, guessed at times, at others misunderstood by the men who created the words: but, in that time, there will no longer be a Science to sum it up, or a person to say it.

Anchored in a phantasmatic that plays off his life and his death throughout those of humanity, Mallarmé's Cratylism proves here to be radical. It is 'modern' in its faith in Science. Yet this faith, which, on the one hand, is nothing but the scarcely concealed trace of negation, is, on the other, offered as a concession. Thus, having provided what he considers adequate guarantees for his adventitious, though contradictory, theses to be acceptable to the positive reader, Mallarmé remains firmly attached to 'ancient subtleties'. The 'Science' that he wishes for, yet dismisses in advance as impossible, is a science that has *already* existed, from Cratylus to de Brosses. Contrary to Saussure, who defined

in advance the future place to be filled by semiology, Mallarmé dreams
instead of reincarnating the memory of a past science: 'In order to
determine the primary and absolutely simple elements of language,
general grammar had to reach back to that imaginary point of contact
where the not yet verbal sound, in a sense, touched upon the actual
vivacity of representation.'[100]

The *Notes* of 1869 situate the moment at the heart of his experience
when, in the course of discovering the linguistics which will free him
from it yet keep it present for him in every word, Mallarmé commits
himself to the path along which he will simultaneously come upon his
poetics and his 'philology': 'To get from the sentence to the *letter*
through the word; using the *Sign* or writing that links the word to its
meaning. Science is therefore nothing other than Grammar, historical
and comparative, in order to become general, and Rhetoric.'[101]

This is a Science which, in all its dimensions, could therefore be
summed up as a meditation upon the isolated graphic sign, the letter-
meaning, that supposedly represents the sound and is indefinitely susceptible to combination. Each ballerina is a sign, and each sign is the
node of a network of meaning – all because *in 'Hérodiade' everything
flashed*. In this sense, Mallarmé's science has always already existed;
its archaic aspect is a ploy: the eighteenth century simply offered a
problematic ready-made for reinvestment by Mallarmé's desire. Neither
past nor future, this is instead an *imaginary* science, entirely isomorphous to the imaginary realm, and completely suited to its needs. It is
here that Mallarmé makes contact with Brisset and Roussel, even
though the results of their identical rediscovery may differ. And this
is certainly why such a science will never be, even though it were some
day again to be possible. Mallarmé says so himself with implacable
rigour: there where it might some day take place, there will have been
nothing but the place, which has always been.

From our present perspective, it suffices to retain from this example
the form of this temptation by the phantasy of *meaning*, doubling
back towards what spawned it: another semiotic order, irrespective of
the historical state of knowledge, is instituted, which distributes the
processes of signification otherwise than his contemporaries imagine.
An *other scene* opens within language, clandestine, withdrawn, melting
in with accepted forms yet corroding them from within, nearly
vampirizing them. New actors are destined for this theatre, delegates
of the double play of the double science: liberated *signifiers* to be
combined.

We can see the outline here of what will become the current pos-
terity for Mallarmé's 'science', once the relation between the signifier
and the signified has again been called into question. Nevertheless, at
this point, Mallarmé has only outlined the prevalence of the signifier;
the interplay between meaning and sound is still supervised, overseen,
on the one hand, by syntax, and, on the other, by that veritable guard-
rail, Science, to which Mallarmé, cautiously, returns:[102]

> What is there? words, first of all: themselves recognizable
> for the letters that compose them, link them and you have
> sentences. A current of intelligence, like a breath, the
> spirit, animates these words, so that several of them express
> a meaning with nuances . . . . The orthographic variations
> of the words, in the jolt given to the reunion of several to
> form a complete meaning, that is, the change in the
> letters determined by the meaning of the sentence, this
> constitutes Grammar, or the formal study of language;
> there remains the material study of the terms themselves,
> isolated and immobile, and this is Lexicography.

The 'spirit' animating these words will be the 'Word' for Brisset,
fiction for Roussel and, for Mallarmé the poet, it will be the Dream;
when he claims only to be a pedagogue, it will be Science – but the one
always shows through the other. Wisely steering mid-way between the
vertigo of the letter and the mystery of total meaning, Mallarmé will
devote himself to the study of words. Thus, each stage of the adventure
will bear a name, and 'science' can also be a harbour; he submits to
chance, the famous chance of the Coup de dés.

Mallarmé will endlessly waver between the Dream, Science, and
word-play. This vacillation will give rise to the poet one day, and the
linguist the next. Even the man about town is subject to these deter-
minants. This can be seen, for example, in the note which he appends
to some Vers de circonstance, entitled 'Easter eggs': 'Each verse was
written in gold ink on a red egg and preceded by a number so as to
reconstitute the quatrain. – A single time, the numbering was able to
be omitted, and, transposing the eggs, the whole thus read several
times in a different way.'[103]

We can reflect upon this symbol (since a verse was also a word for
Mallarmé) which makes him select empty eggs for this ceremonial
combinatory; they are the negatives of the pomegranate in Hérodiade,
which was also red. When the egg is empty, the seed is lost; nothing

such as a 'swarm' could emerge. . . . Thus Mallarmé still might
have been playing with what had been his 'powerlessness'.

He was also concerned with another game in which he had condensed, as with the eggs, the entire meaning of his adventure:[104]

> With extraordinary patience, Mallarmé had built a *Box* for
> learning English through play, and composed only of twelve
> boards of complicated mechanisms for placing automatically,
> before the eyes of the student, questions, answers and the
> coloured images illustrating them.

Here, we can already see Saussure's games, Roussel's novels and Jean
Ferry's machine for reading Roussel, the illuminated vignettes illus-
trating history such as Brisset, bedazzled, *sees* it, and the inferno of
dictionaries and syntax where Wolfson's body will have to circulate.
Hérodiade may well have fallen to the rank of a gadget, but one much
less innocent than it seems.

Having stated what separates Mallarmé from Ducasse, we must now
note certain similarities at the heart of this difference. Whether we are
dealing with one or the other, the signifying processes which they
ultimately privilege (differing by virtue of the very dichotomy produced by Mallarmé: he stresses *words*, whereas Ducasse brings his
efforts to bear on *sentences*), and from which they derive their respective theories, do not fundamentally challenge the conception of the
architectonics of language. They are neither Joyce nor Artaud. They
strive only to discover new possibilities, new dimensions, or strictly
envision taking conscious control of signifying mechanisms or operations that had hitherto remained hidden or neglected. Their respective
philosophical and linguistic antecedents provide the necessary clarifica-
tion. Whereas Ducasse adeptly marks a radical departure from the views
of Port Royal (so radical in fact that Pascal seems suspect), Mallarmé
naturally rejoins (brought there by his phantasy, when the desire to be
'scientific' rivets him to philology) the grammarians of the eighteenth
century, for whom the immanent logic of thought was less important
than the hypothetical 'language of kings' (Jean Roudaut adopts this
expression as the title of the richest chapter in his book).

Despite his *Coup de dés*, Mallarmé respects linguistic order, even
though his writing (in the sense given to this word in the *Notes*) works
at softening it, distending it, musicalizing it. This is none the less an

unorthodox desire; it gives rise to 'poetic' phenomena that will regularly and constantly associate themselves with any experience with language seeking to bring forth – either against or through established knowledge – its unsuspected laws. From this point of view, Derrida is no further from Fabre d'Olivet than Joyce is from Mallarmé. The difference between Joyce and Mallarmé, however, is that the latter, even in giving play to the sentence, maintains its ordinary rules. He does not seek to unleash infinite expenditure or its reserves. Language presupposes a law designed to measure the limits of a certain freedom; to exceed those limits is to end up *elsewhere*. Whether Delirium or Reason (assuming such a distinction can even have a meaning), the works of Roussel, Brisset and quite a few others will always be *regulated* – and could not exist without the rules that inform even their merest traits. Delineating the field under the jurisdiction of laws; causing play to be presided over by the agency of Science (and not just any Science: linguistics); restraining a fascinating sensation of danger, tied to the illumination of a discovered secret – these are the characteristics common to the research of all *logophiles*.

2 The sign: wisdom and madness

Reinvesting itself in the discourses of tradition, and making word-play the new outlet for what remains that old myth, Poetry, Mallarmé's madness is converted into mere daring. The fiction that results from breaking the simple rhythms of the sign becomes abstracted in a spectacle where dancing concepts supplant that flesh and blood dancer, Hérodiade. The resurgence of the Dream is no more than a pool of echoes, henceforth illegible forms without contours. An enforced forgetfulness has cost him the *vision*. Mallarmé's prudence will not give in to the 'true' spectacles derived by Roussel from the same sources, and carried by the flow of waters or across the weave of a cloth being made in *Impressions d'Afrique*.

We must abandon Mallarmé at the point when something in him succumbs, when he again submits to literary ideology – 'I become once more a pure and simple writer of literature.' He nevertheless remains the one who taught us what we do not know about the 'madness' of Roussel, Saussure and Brisset – and for this we owe him homage. He alone makes it possible for us to understand how a delirium and a writing, a vision and a science can be bound up in an experience which he was able to inscribe and preserve. Thanks to him, the link between the sign and fiction in the field of desire takes on both form and meaning, and compels a dissolution of those distinctions that seek to uphold the autonomous purity of constituted discursive fields: poetry on one side, linguistics on the other, with their remainder and supplement simply designated as 'fiction'. A dynamic that disrupts genealogies becomes visible: poetry is not born simply from poetry, nor science from science, nor the novel from phantasy. We can detect numerous links weaving an unknown network, irrigated by the desire that gave birth to it.

There is a 'non-knowledge' to be unearthed. But how?

Our only means of reaching it is through the *sign*. As we have seen, Mallarmé's entire experience played itself out in the detours of his encounter with that being which was not yet for him a concept; it was a word, a sound, a letter, impossible, unthinkable objects, scenic loci of his inner theatre. Only later would he be able to integrate all this in a knowledge that could be shared with others, a *linguistics* which permitted him to limit and contain the incomprehensible source of his 'decomposition'. Henceforth, the word 'sign' would become his guard-rail, the ramp separating the scene from reason, the means to a mastery that would make poetry a restrained economy: the bleeding of meaning, of expenditure, is definitively throttled. The sovereignty of the Tournon nights is now no more than mastery, craft.

The sign is also a shoreline; it is a theoretical object that equips us with a retrospective knowledge through which the drift makes sense. And we have gathered this knowledge from Mallarmé at the conclusion of an adventure he denies. If we know today what a sign is – albeit a stumbling knowledge – we owe it in part to Mallarmé who permits us to understand that no sign is pure or innocent. The sign only becomes an instrument, a formal order, against the backdrop of a history. Even as a concept, the sign always conceals a 'madness' of thought which finally submits to its order.

We say today that the sign made this madness possible, but this is incomplete: 'madness' is what allows us to grasp the contour of the sign's immaterial being. From this standpoint, our knowledge depends upon another experience which completes Mallarmé's, namely that of Saussure. Mallarmé lives madness and through it discovers the *experience* of the sign; for him, it is still an imprecise object to be used for making poetry. But it is Saussure who produces the *concept* of the sign; he completes its science after having himself lived the madness of the sign, but already from the *very interior* of the science which he could then constitute. The poetry through which Saussure's madness is revealed is the poetry of others (Saturnian, Vedic hymns, Lucretius, etc.), and this madness is possible only from within a knowledge which he is not alone in producing. In a certain sense, what goes mad, in Saussure, is science. Linguistics itself harbours the madness which makes the 'anagrams' possible. Linguistic science will henceforth *control* the delirium inherent to any language by attempting to separate the *system* from the *subject*. Desperately, Wolfson would prove this to himself.

From this encounter, the movement of our research can be outlined on the one hand because the concept of the sign exists, and
because this has not been achieved without a detour through a certain
madness; on the other hand because it enables us to understand an
even greater madness, namely Mallarmé's, by demonstrating what
happens *when it does not yet exist*, but already allows itself to be
anticipated. From Mallarmé to Saussure, the entire enigma of our
modernity takes shape. It is the modernity of linguistic reason inciting
and repressing madness, liberating and chaining desire, producing and
analysing fiction. The very mark of our time is to perform all this in
a solitary gesture that always passes through the mysterious knot of
the sign, between knowledge and delirium. If we have said that
Mallarmé inaugurates our epoch, we must add that it is Saussure who
completes it. The experience of the one and the knowledge of the
other define the configuration of what is still today the exclusive field
of the sign. The labour of Roussel, the apotheosis of Brisset, the
wandering of Wolfson have no *meaning* except in this field, and no
possibility except those of the sign. And, as we shall see, the fact that,
at one time or another, each reverts to an outmoded knowledge
(eighteenth-century linguistics), itself makes no sense except in
reference to what made this a marginal science.

We may thus venture forth again from the *sign,* since we now know
where we learned what we know of it. Returning from Idumaea,
Mallarmé brings back intact what had never left him: his pre-theoretical
practice of the sign. The two planes, of expression and content, remain
firmly established in what is both an irreducible distance and an in-
violable proximity; this has endured despite new suggestions concerning
the Dream, which continue to provide glimpses of the threat he once
faced of being swallowed up by 'Nothingness'. The network of the
signifier has acquired a certain, limited freedom: the elements of each
of the two planes of the sign have discretely displaced the foundations
of their interrelation, and begun to play with the instituted tolerances
which guarantee their interdependence and lability.
In his poetry as in his prose, Mallarmé explores spaces that have
become abstract, and whose rules remain to be formulated. But Mallarmé's experience contributes to the appearance of the outline of
these rules in an anonymous theoretical consciousness that will eventually determine and articulate them. Mallarmé's entire experience
leans towards Saussure's science but, inversely, Saussure's science must

31

make a preliminary detour through something which closely resembles the Mallarméan experience itself.

In Saussure's theoretical practice, the axial concept of the arbitrariness of the sign only appears as the *remainder*, the precipitate of a practice within language such as only the absence of this theory could have authorized. The emergence of the theory depends upon the latter practice; in the global economy which they form, together, the theory has the primary function of repressing the still clandestine practice, through the inevitable mode of negation. The apparently theoretical experience of the *anagrams*, which hinges upon the *letter* (in the evidently pre-Saussurian sense which Mallarmé gave to this word), is in fact and above all a savage textual practice, an adventure with unfathomable surprises across the black continent of languages.

The autonomy of the signifier is the unformulated postulate which permits and generates the entire undertaking; because, in the anagrams notebooks, the phoneme is now no more than the multi-sided unity of a particular system of accounting (whence the meditation on the *Stab* of the ancient Germans). Although unthematized, this is a prodigious 'discovery' that, as we shall see, produces remarkable effects of fiction. In the end, terrified at having come upon his madness, Saussure will question his discovery. But to exorcize it, there will have to appear, with all its concision and contours, the theory of the sign, necessarily linked to the sequestration of the signifier via its inscription in the closure of the system of the language.

The infinite opening of language by the anagram upon the imaginary, fiction and all other languages will give way to an opening measured in terms of real history – the only truly attested one. The anagram was the ahistorical vertigo of a language unfurling its possibilities in the instantaneity of an individual imagination; on the contrary, structural linguistics works to reduce the individual by adopting the time of History as its only horizon. The enclosure of the sign in the system of language recapitulates the one which designates and contains madness. Touched upon then refused by Saussure in the name of the new science, madness will henceforth be the sole predicate of semiotic freedom – lest an '*avant-garde*' get involved with it.

Saussure thus withdraws to a terrain marked off by reason (against madness and for rationality), under the cover of *science*. As for Mallarmé, his knowledge will be his refuge regained; but the *language* that he takes with him as a theoretical object, will be no more than the symbol of his foresworn desire. Taking the side of Hermogenes against Cratylus (if we transpose their debate to the discussion of the relation between the signifier and the signified), Saussure condemns as deviant and as powerless to produce positive knowledge all semiotic practices which henceforth disregard the Sr/Sd split and the 'convention' governing it, in the interest of facilitating a connection between their semiosis and the flux of desire.

Saussure repeats, scarcely outlined, the first step he braved, and the threshold where he hesitates will henceforth mark the frontier where meaning and reason culminate together: the symbolic order which permits the embodiment of a speech that can be designated as full or empty. Abandoning anagrams, Saussure thus produces the very possibility for psychiatry to find a bedrock of positivities in the rela-tion between the subject and language – in spite of counter-claims by the few whose truth is not satisfied by this order. The latter do not hesitate to engage in profound rearrangements of the rules which the symbolic order imposes as limits; for them there remain other, possible rules which they will not allow to be suppressed. Roussel explores these other rules, the *other* of rules, in order to make our world a simulacrum of the fiction contained – enveloped and held back – by words. Brisset, the grammarian of the hidden slope of languages, remains the pure theoretician of these rules; but he goes beyond them to explore their depth in real fictions, whereas Wolfson flees and finds himself as he slides indefinitely on their unlimited surface. Each in his own way risks the adventure by variously retouching the vessel on which he travels; but, in so doing, they all indicate a cut, a breach, an ineradicable flaw in what upholds our world, and thereby bring forth a new horizon from the ancient territory. Deleuze and Guattari offer a glimpse of this 'deterritorialization of enunciation' through which a new subject is invented.

The language of psychoanalysis, as a theory of the signifier and of desire, itself produced in a sense by these encounters between language and madness, permits us to state the meaning of all these adventures – permits, that is, to the extent that these texts can be *read*, and accord-ing to their own logic. This logic is that of the 'madness' which inhabits language *and* its science. Any research upon language thus has madness as a border. This is because language is the locus of meaning in its sociality; to disarticulate languages is necessarily to disarticulate the institutional economy of univocal and repressive meaning – and to bring forth what *speaks in them* and *against* them: the truth of desire. Because it is articulated, there is nothing more fragile than the sign, nothing more distressing than its permanent and menacing gap. The sign is the weakest link in the symbolic order; the Cratylistic impulse in each of us is the infinite effort to suture the split in the sign in order to find meaning and delight. Even Socrates, playing Cratylus' game, surrenders to the intoxication of the sign and describes that inexplicable 'wisdom which instantaneously comes to him' from analysing the name of the gods.

Wisdom and madness, what is born of the encounter between the sign and desire produces both delight and anguish, despair and hope. The despair and the anguish brought forth by the void discovered at the heart of the sign are invested with a peculiar prescience that gives rise to the menacing figure of *power*. For Plato, it is the power of the gods, who perhaps play with men, or the power of the Legislator in his senseless intoxication; for Piis, it is the 'Langue of Kings'; for Brisset, the savage arbitrariness of politicos, priests and academies – not to mention the luxurious and sadistic desires of the gods and demons; Roussel introduces knowledge and power to his novels, and blends them in the language machine; as for Wolfson, isn't it the despotism of his mother and his psychiatrist that he must endlessly flee and counteract? Even Saussure, in search of the lost historical truth of his anagrams, is in turn compelled to suppose the existence of an occult caste of literati, in league with each other throughout the pyramid of powers.

Yet, in compensation, there does remain an indestructible hope, the outlet for a delight that is still possible. Plato's men can still rely on their reason; Brisset hopes for the future fraternity promised by God; Roussel, throughout all his setbacks, believes in future success, in the fraternity of the writers who will come after him and who will understand the value of his procedure; Wolfson roams through Manhattan and even finds a fraternal prostitute; Saussure believes in the solidarity of poets.

As schizophrenics they are carried away by the drift, allowing their flux to wander across the full body of language; as paranoiacs, they endlessly pursue the schism in order to reinvent history as the history of desire, building their empire of science and text. But, whatever their clinical fate, they are above all the witnesses of a unique experience, the 'mad' adventures of a world that we did not suspect, lying in wait in the sign.

3 The power of Babel*

Enlightenment

For us, everything always begins (and this is the origin of the narrative as a narrative of the origin) with a sudden break which announces itself – absolute origin, irreducible beginning – as the epiphany of a new structure in the movement of an instantaneous revelation. A new *meaning* presents itself in a total rearrangement of everything we thought we knew. A *vision* is encountered at the outcome of a *research*. For the encounter is never fortuitous: first there was the enigma of a problem without a solution, the disappointed desire for an outlet, a belabouring that affects the entire network of a problematic whose unproductive blockage points to the insufficiencies of a knowledge. The end of the research becomes a requirement to go beyond. The enlightenment of the logophile is above all an operation which affects the very axes of his concrete gnoseological process. In this sense, the experience of the discontinuity which suddenly remodels the conditions for a knowledge is known by every 'seeker' – whether he seeks the path of wisdom, the solution to a practical or epistemological problem, or even the first verse of a poem or the missing rule in a theoretical structure. This is a well-known phenomenon, which A. Koestler called *Eureka feeling*, and which Archimedes symbolizes. The blinding flash associated with it is necessary for a paradigm of the 'normal science' to resolve its contradictions in the discontinuity which forms the 'extraordinary science' and produces a new paradigm (cf. Kuhn, Lakatos). The instantaneous operation first produces a *vision*, which contains the future spread out in a simultaneity in which all the possibilities of an immense combinatory exist on the same plane; this is the anticipated course of a potentially inexhaustible production, none the less exhausted by the

35

vision. All of a sudden, the subject, who had been knocking against the impasses of his problem as against the limits of himself, the confines of his finitude, launches into a new plenitude.

Mallarmé had 'dredged the verse' in every sense when his vision of Dream and Horror appeared. An identical situation befell Roussel, and a similar one Brisset, trying to resolve the logical aporias of his grammatical taxonomy. Saussure as well struggled with the Saturnian enigma, and Wolfson wanted to survive, against words. Enlightenment is the sphinx overcome, and the entire experience of each follows each phase of the myth; it is a question of life or death, sanctioned by the reward of a hitherto forbidden knowledge. Only then will the vision have to be put to the test, and verified or proven according to the technological rationality of a *procedure* – which promises to involve a protracted labour.

The Saussure of the anagrams notebooks travelled this path, perhaps more than once; the first time, of which we know nothing, may have been at the origin of the *Thesis on the primitive system of vowels in European languages.* What he says there of his discovery seems to describe in slow motion the very process of rearrangement which makes up the core of enlightenment:[1]

> To study the multiple forms under which what we call the
> Indo-European *a* manifests itself, this is the immediate
> object of this treatise: the other vowels will only be taken
> into consideration in so far as phenomena related to the *a*
> will provide the occasion. But if, having reached the edge
> of the field thus circumscribed, the tableau of Indo-European
> vocalism has modified itself little by little before our eyes,
> and we see it entirely grouped around, and taking a new atti-
> tude with regard to the *a*, it is clear that the system of vowels
> as a whole will have entered into the scope of our observation,
> and its name must be inscribed on the first page.

We, likewise, know nothing of the process whereby Saussure came to discover, in 1889, a 'bizarre' law designed to classify 'certain details of Homeric versification' (lecture at the Linguistic Society of Paris[2]). We shall come back to it, as the problem of the anagrams is already posed there in a certain way. We do know, however, from Saussure's letters to Meillet, that his discovery of these anagrams did follow the model for all enlightenment:

I can announce to you that victory is now mine along the

front. I spent two months questioning the monster and
groping my way towards him, but for three days I have
been advancing with heavy artillery.[3]

The entire phenomenon of alliteration (and also of rhymes)
that we noted in the Saturnian is but an insignificant part
of a more general phenomenon, or rather of an *absolutely
total* one.[4]

Saussure himself takes up the theme of the Sphinx in his allusion
to the 'monster' that he had to question, effecting here the remarkable
reversal of roles so common to logophiles; Mallarmé had also spoken to
his correspondents of the 'monster' he had to face. But Mallarmé had
plunged into his discovery following this first moment of revelation in
which everything lines up beneath the same law in the very moment
when the field of its application is disclosed. Saussure, however, will
only pursue his first vision with extreme caution, but not without
great impatience. If he does not throw himself like others into the
gaping breach, it is perhaps because he only succeeded in forcing it
through the path of institutional paranoia known as the scientific
method: he needs *proof* of the glimpsed truth. This surely betrays a
misunderstanding of the profound character of enlightenment, in so
far as the discovered truth is nothing but proof of a truth of the subject.

Because the 'proof' demanded by Saussure's scientific super-ego
could not be cornered, he could only remain on the terrain where such
a requirement was law, in the lap of Science. Two years after his
experience, Saussure would declare himself 'perplexed' by 'what to
think of the reality of the phantasmagoria of the entire affair'.[5] Mean-
while, this certainty never quite acquired, this anxiety never quite
sutured, will have brought forth that mad text: the Saturnian fiction.

Roussel, however, wished for the survival of a trace which attested
to the reality of his enlightenment; he even took the care to cite the
observations which Janet had made upon his case, in that testament-
like documentary entitled *How I Wrote Some of My Books*. For him,
enlightenment is the moment in which he discovers the truth of his
destiny in a total fusion of his body with that of writing:[6]

I would like to note here a curious crisis which I underwent
at the age of nineteen, when I was writing *La Doublure*. For
several months I experienced an extraordinarily intense
sensation of universal glory. Dr Pierre Janet, who cared for

me for long years, has described this crisis in the first volume
of his work De L'Angoisse à L'Extase . . . .

As François Caradec rightly observes, 'for Raymond Roussel, time
stopped in 1896',[7] the date of the crisis and of La Doublure: he will
place a photograph from this period as a frontispiece to How I Wrote
Some of My Books (1935), with the caption: 'Raymond Roussel at
nineteen, while he was writing La Doublure'. The same photo was also
to have served as a model for the statue – never completed – with
which he had planned to adorn his funeral monument. Extraordinary
fidelity to the gift of revelation.

In the pages of the Janet study that Roussel chose to reproduce,
details are given as to the content and forms of the 'crisis' lived so
intensely by Roussel; in particular, he quotes this sentence, which has
since become famous: 'Yes, I once felt that I had a star on my brow,
and I will never forget it.'[8]

As the title of one of Roussel's plays, Star on the Brow would mark
the profound link between writing and the divine moment of ecstasy.
Dreaming of himself as a statue, perhaps, Roussel identifies with a new
Moses descending from Sinai; with rays of light beaming from his brow
and his arm holding the Decalogue: the very symbol of the sacred
character of every writing. Perhaps this even has some relation to the
Moses that questioned Freud, Michelangelo's, at San Pietro in Vincoli.
Let us not forget that the photograph so dear to Roussel was taken
during a trip to Italy with his mother. Moses is another face of the
Sphinx.

As for the play whose title recalls the ecstasy, it is not the simple
account of such an event, but rather its exploration; it is a subtle and
minute investigation of the nuances of the 'gift' in its relation to the
activity of writing: a staging of phantasy represented through the use of
the very method of delirium, because the text derives in fact from the
same 'procedure' as Impressions of Africa. The entire play thus functions as the illustration of its own truth, by repeating the work of its
origin: the signified reflects and utters the signifying law which makes
it possible.

But the phenomenon of the doubling of representations would play
the role of producing and regulating texts in all of Roussel's work:
problems of splitting, of repetition, of duplication. The mystery of the
double haunts both the narratives and the procedure, as the latter would
have recourse to complex techniques of coupling. The obsession for

alliteration in Mallarmé, its generalization in the theory of anagrams by
Saussure and Brisset, the search for equivalences between phonic series
by Wolfson – all these phenomena are notably bound to the symptom
they all underwent, but for which Roussel provided a particularly
clear thematization in composing a piece whose very title indicates
its privilege as a cross-roads:[9]

> One day at the age of seventeen, I opted to abandon music
> in favour of writing only verse; my vocation had been
> decided. From that moment a fever of work took hold of
> me. I worked, so to speak, night and day for long months,
> at the end of which I wrote *La Doublure*, the composition
> of which coincides with the crisis described by Pierre
> Janet.

The notion of 'dissociation of the personality', which Kraepelin
might have used, can only mark one aspect of the experience, as it
neglects the conditions indissociable from its emergence: *work within
writing*. The dissociation is, as it were, turned back, recovered and
reinvested in the very thematics and texture of the texts, which accom-
pany its apparition and benefit from the unfurling of energy suddenly
released. This last feature is also shared by all enlightened logophiles.
The example of Roussel shows fairly well what energetic power suddenly erupts in the apparatus of writing; it is sufficiently vigorous to
fuel an activity of indefinite duration, because the time of the vision
is the synchrony of a system to be crossed, without regard for other
realities. Mallarmé also knew that he had given himself, at Tournon,
enough work for the rest of his life. This was also literally true of
Brisset and of Wolfson, and is perfectly manifest in the inexhaustible
series of analyses in Saussure's anagram notebooks. The fission of the
sign, unlike that of the atom, can be controlled: the spark is prolonged,
the expenditure through *cathexis* never stops depleting itself; the
structure of its temporality is the eternity of the instant.

The energy suddenly made available arms the logophile with a
definite power; the sentiment of omnipotence bursts forth in Roussel,
is evident in Saussure's military metaphors (cf. the Meillet letter cited
above), is manifest in Mallarmé gliding high above humanity, and is
also present throughout Brisset's work. Wolfson's account of his 'discovery' (which only concerns one 'procedure' but which will accord
him the pleasure of numerous encounters – indefinite reliance upon
the same intuition) presents, although not without humour, its flash:

'in spite of his apparent incapacity, the psychotic had, perhaps, it was rather vague, an inordinate sense of his own competence. At times he even had the sense of being able to do anything in any speciality whatever if only he wanted to . . . .'[10]

The psychoanalytic thesis concerning the role of narcissism in psychosis finds here a perfect illustration. The omnipotence experienced by Wolfson should by rights have made any career – and perhaps all of them – available to him; such was the dictate of his enlightenment. None the less – and psychoanalysis does not foresee this particularity – Wolfson does not opt for just 'any' career; nor could it evidently be the pure resolution of a sovereign free will that drives him to engage his entire reserve of previously unsuspected strengths, precisely and as if by chance, in the study of language: 'the schizophrenic suddenly became enthralled by the study of languages . . . .'[11] Unwittingly, he thus takes to the same path as all the others before him: Mallarmé, Saussure, Brisset, Roussel . . . . It should be carefully noted, however, that it is a question *of individual languages* [des langues] and not *of language* [du langage]; we shall see what meaning is reserved for this exclusive attention, which seems to foreclose – in the strongest sense – any consideration of a general impact upon the faculty of language itself. Here is one of the most apparent limits of modern logophilia, when compared to the 'semisophia' of the eighteenth century, whose primary emphasis was the very origin of language. It was a question then of research designed to yield a universalizing synthesis: man was to be *generated*, as a social being, who had language and produced knowledge. Yet, the logophile is interested only in genesis – or more precisely, in the rebirth of his self. To question language, for him, is to question himself as a subject. Thus, *language* as a formal, *a priori* condition for the humanity of man never becomes an object of study: it seems to follow. The individual language (*la langue*) alone is the target – but even less as a specific national tongue than for its general characteristics as a concrete system of articulation. It is typical that Brisset becomes a philologist, who formally inscribes in his system the possibility for all natural languages to state the same proofs according to the same procedures. Mallarmé starts with the same premises in the *Mots anglais* in meditating upon the phonemes independently of the system of each language. Wolfson evidently follows the same path: 'Thus, fascinated with the study of languages after his last escape from the hospital, he decided more or less to perfect his knowledge of the two Germanic and Romance tongues . . .'[12] (German and French)

For him, this means above all an end to the suffering inflicted by his every transaction with his maternal tongue – because it is the language which his mother persists in speaking to him: English. Wolfson's primary motivations do not strictly coincide with those of the other logophiles, at least not at the most apparent level, and this is an indication of the diacritical value of their respective attitudes towards the problem of natural languages. In fact, Saussure never seeks to export his discovery beyond the domain of Latin, and he even renounces his research into Latin literature at the end of a few years; Roussel restricts his application to French, and his procedure is, after all, but one of the possibilities of composition foreseen by his methodology; Mallarmé ostensibly segregates his research into English from his poetic work – despite their real ties. Consequently, one can only note a significant correlation between the degree of severity of the 'psychic disorders' and the number of natural languages invested by the logophile: Wolfson takes a sampling from several linguistic families, while Brisset extends his theory, at least in principle, to all possible languages.

It should therefore come as no surprise that Brisset was, of them all, the one who experienced enlightenment in its purest form, and on several occasions. His repeated references to it in his works stress the determinant value of these recurring events:

> The light flashed . . . ;[13] a truth which dazzles us;[14] light came
> to us so intensely . . .[15] What immense emotion we felt when
> these scenes presented themselves to our spirit!;[16] The fever of
> the spirit allows us no rest. We write under its inspiration to
> find it;[17] We were positively terrified at the hands of an irres-
> tible power.[18]

Furthermore, it is he who proclaims: 'It is a madness abandoned to enlightened spirits! You said it! It is an enlightened spirit who speaks to you.'[19]

More passive, and thoroughly impregnated with religion, Brisset does not doubt for an instant that the light he receives comes from the spirit. This reveals another differentiating modality which could help us to grasp the meaning of the different deliria. Everything takes place as if the core of what each logophile believed before the crisis had displaced itself in the course of this experience in order to occupy, intact, a preponderant place in the structure of the delirium. More precisely, where a *belief* and a *practice* coexisted without manifest relation to

one another before the crisis, there appears after the crisis a new organization which places the pre-existing belief in the position of a *theory*
for his practice. If Brisset analyses the 'Word', it is because, from the
outset, he believes in an evangelical God whose existence guarantees
and justifies all his research. What, for Brisset, is truly a matter of
'belief', may only be for the others a certain mode of investing a prior
knowledge that has not, or has scarcely been theorized. With the essential fact being the promotion of the belief or 'theory' to a primary
status, each delirium can be differentiated in function of its intrinsic
nature. In the cases which concern us, the prior belief *always* has some
relation to language (God as Verb for Brisset; the mother as the subject
of English for Wolfson, etc.), and the same applies to what we have
called the 'practice': Mallarmé writes verse, Saussure is a linguist, etc.

Brisset nevertheless represents an extreme case, in so far as he does
not relate back to himself the belief which has become theory and
source of all knowledge as well as the justification for his entire practice: the enlightenment is lived for him through aspects of the *other*, a
presence from without with whom he holds a dialogue, repeating the
prophets. But he does not take long to discover that the exterior from
which the other addresses him is nothing but his own interiority;
consequently, he *is* himself the other who speaks to him. Yet, instead
of returning the other to himself, instead of closing the space of the
delirium by unifying the speech which proffers it, it is himself as subject that Brisset projects into the prophetic figure of his estrangement,
aspired to by his own miraculous excrescence: he *becomes* the
'seventh angel'. Mallarmé, himself, who had become 'impersonal', as
he stated in a letter, was for a time Nothingness. Wolfson was too busy
slipping on the Moebius strip of languages even to be able to pose the
problem of his subjectivity: from the outset, he is an other; the proof
is that he systematically refers to himself in the third person and, in so
doing, uses a term borrowed from the discourse of the knowledge
which oppresses him: 'the schizophrenic'. As for Saussure and Roussel,
they never doubt that the knowledge which serves them is truly their
own: this sense of the property of knowledge is the immediate foundation for the remaining 'self': a purely epistemological subjectivity that
proves itself by remaining operational.

To a certain extent, Brisset, as well, retains this fundamental certainty. Neither the reality of the experience he lived, nor the conviction
that he is the only prophet to manifest a certain truth, prevents his
remaining a positivist to the depths of his delirium. Like Saussure, he

believes in the 'proof'. Where they differ, however, is that, instead of setting himself the task of providing proof for his claims. Brisset settles for awaiting an impossible denial, that he is prepared to defy. His assurance has an admirable quality: 'If the answers that have inspired us are those of a madman, they will be easy to refute.'[20]

Brisset's sacred epistemology anticipates the principles of modern science, which recognizes the value of 'falsification', but no longer believes in simple 'verification'. Brisset's faith in the profound identity of the Word, of reason and of science is a revival of the entire *logos*. In fact, it is through this conviction that Brisset surrenders to his madness, in the belief that he is protected from it. Believing that he has eliminated from his theories every incidence of belief and madness, he rejects them both; but, in so doing, he refers to the very logic of the anagram, and listens to the suggestions of paronomasis (in the manner of Mallarmé, who linked the *'fiole'* of *Igitur*'s suicide to *'folie'*) – 'faith [*la foi*] and madness [*la folie*] are sisters'.[21] Because he hates all forms of established religion, because he considers himself exempt from vulgar 'faith', and because, to him, 'faith' and 'madness' are the same thing, he could not possibly be mad. Madness plays a dirty trick on Brisset by making him believe that it does not exist, when it is responsible for dictating to him the words used to 'prove' its non-existence.

Given the very object of his reasoning, Brisset reveals here an essential trait of logophilia: on the one hand, it inevitably leads to the banks of madness, but, on the other, itself poses madness as a criterion for the validity of its theses. Whence the ambivalence of the role of the 'proof', which is as responsible for proving the absence of madness as the reality of a law. Here, Brisset follows, in his own way, the traces of Descartes, for whom it was equally essential, before anything else, to prove the reality of his reason. Only their methods differ, but that is the key factor: Brisset wants to prove his reason from the *interior* of his madness. He is alone in such 'illogism' – which may explain the minor importance (if not the total absence) of the relation between proof and madness in the other deliria examined here.

For Brisset, the common anchoring for the terms 'Faith' and 'Madness' is marked by the play of signifiers whose similitude (*foi/folie*) guarantees the real identity of their referents. But this example also shows that, for the logophile, everything which starts from language, returns to it. Brisset says as much, again in his own way, but in a way that all descendants of Cratylus – including Freud – could accept as valid: 'I am *Pi*, *ar* which moves back, *ole* which moves forward.'[22]

The play which undoes the *Word* (*P-ar-ole*) to discover what it means, by looking beneath the signifier for other signifiers whose signifieds will precisely analyse the first signified, this play which wants to know what *every word* says, puts its chips on the table: it has the logic of a phantasy and the locus of a desire. Though diversely appreciated in different circumstances, these are the stakes of every Cratylism. Whether it is called 'science' or 'philosophy' when the research is that of a collectivity, or 'delirium' or 'madness' when the research is an individual matter. In the case of logophiles, the distinction between science and madness depends upon the location of the discourse with regard to the social complex. What was legitimate research for de Brosses was proof of dementia in Brisset. And yet, for one as for the other, it was a question of the very possibility for *meaning* to disclose and justify itself in the texture of its manifestation. This texture, this galaxy of signifiers, thus becomes the pure, immanent origin, the infinite structure of references in which meaning finds nothing but itself, without fail, without loss, without a breach where nonsense might remain possible: signifieds as far as the eye can see, as long as there is breath.

To go this far, and to do so in spite of the implicit acknowledgment of a level at which the signifier possesses a formal existence of its own, one must radically deny the independence of the latter, on the grounds that it is fictitious, painful or dangerous: any floating signifier is forcefully reintegrated to the closed orbit of meaning. If need be, the signifier can even be dislocated, and submitted to a variety of recombinations affecting its elementary components. Yet, for this to be possible, the sign initially had to burst, and the signifier and signified had in some way to be recognized in all their 'arbitrary distance'. But this operation is but a *moment* that is never susceptible to theorization, lest language plummet into non-signifying exteriority, dragging with it the subject henceforth deprived of his foundations. The distance from the signifier to the signified, their relative indifference, are thus denied at the very moment at which they are implicitly supposed and necessary to the decorum of the delirium. The signified at once sets in motion an endless, ever-changing parade of signifiers, as if language had staggered and displaced everything, and established resemblances as a basis for reconstructing real genealogies. The entire language becomes a rebus, a puzzle, proposed by a good or crafty genie, a sphinx whose question remains deadly.

The sign thus re-forms in a paradoxical fiction, in which the subject may finally locate himself without fear of again becoming lost: through the glimmer, the incandescent dust of the words, he has but to dip into the infinity of a meaning irrigating language, becoming its very matter, the substance of a truth, the narrative of a History, the figure of a God or of a self – 'It is God himself who will speak to you.'[23] The semiotic chaos becomes a divine cosmos. Isn't this what Socrates implied when, beneath the name of the gods, *theous*, he read *theontas*, 'those who run', namely 'the celestial bodies' – galaxy of signifiers, submerged in the plenitude of the meaning which coincides with them and inexhaustibly runs throughout language without depleting the words?

This uncovers the limit of what is taught by enlightenment: at the moment when the world and language are indistinguishable, the subject who has converted one into the other becomes god. Not everyone's desire is equal to such an apotheosis. At the moment when Brisset discovers himself as the god of his enthusiasm, Socrates has already hesitated, and relegated madness to *another* imprecise category, knowledge, which he had dismissed at the beginning of his investigation; now, he recalls it, stating that we know nothing of the gods, especially not the names they use to address each other; let us keep to the things we know with certitude. This is the very gesture of Mallarmé, who suddenly feels the need to regain the ground of science to escape the appeal of his 'Dream'; it is also that of Saussure who reverts to statistics to get away from the question of the existence or the non-existence of the anagrams – all the while taking care to await the response.

The apotheosis promised to the speaker, who speaks *of* Speech *within* speech, is thus blocked, repressed, prohibited beneath the specious naturalness of a system that closes like an Eden from which no further attempt at escape is permitted: the system of the language, the system to which cautious Hermogenes withdraws because he doesn't want to know any more about it. It is because, says Socrates, 'if someone persists in analysing names into words, and inquiring of the elements forming these words, and constantly repeats the process, the one who must answer must finally abandon the inquiry, in despair.'[24]

Etymologies will always be the agonizing reverse of Cratylism because they endlessly entail raising the question of the origin. All language thus becomes essentially 'uncanny', up to the moment when philological science is sufficiently sure of itself to put a firm stop to any expansion of fiction. There is no small irony in the fact that it is Saussure who writes, for example, in 1906, that is to say at the very moment when his research into anagrams was apparently beginning:

'This is an undertaking which could in general be accused, in etymology, of being a rather pitiful game, to take on limpid forms in the interest of finding something other than what they present at face value.'[25] But this doesn't prevent his adding:[26]

> But the ingeniousness of popular etymologies equals or exceeds those of grammarians, and this is a factor which should never be completely forgotten. This would lead to commiting inverse errors. Whereas they may occasionally settle for an imperfect result . . . , the small miracles accomplished elsewhere through this principle can fascinate the linguist, and thoroughly mislead him at each instant.

With his anagrams, Saussure had no objective other than to repeat this gesture of popular etymology, 'fascinated' as he was by the powers of his science. It may not be indifferent to note that the theme of the article quoted above is tied to the traditions concerning Demeter and Eleusis, and speaks of grains and seeds: metaphors for the generative signifier. Yet Saussure never lets himself be carried away to the same extremities as Brisset, and prefers discouragement to apotheosis; he abandons his anagrams and takes refuge in the shelter of a closure he has just erected, that of the linguistic system he 'invents'. His gesture amounts to the creation of an *outside* of language, and of an *exteriority* within it, since the sign will have to be distinguished from the referent, and, within the sign, the signified from the signifier. Yet, for a long period of time, he had believed that everything was only an interior without exterior, or rather a continuous surface, that could be neither right-side-up nor upside-down; the Latin corpus of the anagrams was a torus with unattainable limits, as were languages in general for Brisset, French for Roussel, and a few selected languages for Wolfson. What the logophiles thus assume with regard to language would seem to coincide with what Lacan discovers about the structure of the subject. Language is the reverse of the body, the soul turned inside out. In this image which no mirror returns, the subject can only see the blessing of a god or the scowl of a demon.

Panglossia

Saussure eludes madness, Mallarmé pulls free of it. Roussel settles into a folly that his environment and public rumour naturalize as 'eccentricity'. Wolfson drifts away and Brisset disappears. We have seen nevertheless that their common *experience* possesses a structure and determinations that are identical, when considered in the light of certain essential traits. But we have also seen that the *modalities* of the experience, its concrete content, the knowledge and practices that nourish it, cannot in any case be reduced to a single model. In spite of numerous similarities, Brisset's enlightenment is not Mallarmé's ecstasy. The final outcome of each delirium is doubtless dictated from the beginning by the configuration of the relation between knowledge and practice, on the basis of which each delirium develops in its specificity. Therein lies a logic inherent to fictions which gives them a precise form – or rather assigns them limits and fields which the logophile is powerless to transgress. Everything takes place as if each were to explore to the end all the ramifications of the path disclosed by his enlightenment – and nothing else. In the very particular case of the logophiles, the *knowledge* with which they set out will be both what authorizes the expansion of a scientific fiction into delirium, and what imposes, from the outset, limits that the logophile will not be able to go beyond. Mallarmé begins with the verse, and returns to it; Roussel begins with words, and never again leaves them; Wolfson remains within language in general as the locus for the possibility of being a subject; Saussure begins with linguistics, and rediscovers it – albeit disordered. Brisset alone goes beyond, but in our estimation only because for him nothing differentiates language from the Word. Each delirium thus obtains its characteristics from a certain relation to limits that are also the conditions of its possibility. 'Madness' is not singular; it is not ruled by arbitrariness – but it does possess the equivalent of a 'fatality' of structure.

Thus, Saussure is able to avoid madness, but not through a remnant of reason, a final cautious reflex at the point of succumbing, or some lucky happenstance; his delirium has 'natural' limits because it was already confined to a field circumscribed by immovable frontiers that had been set once and for all. Here, the delirium conforms to the very rules of the scientific method: a problem is posed in a perfectly defined domain, on the basis of a precise theory and according to codified rules. To fail to reinscribe any result in the initial paradigm would be to deprive it of *meaning*. The only alternative, if the paradigm proves insufficient, consists of switching to another. This may be where the difference lies: the structure of a paradigm may be disrupted, whereas the problematic of a delirium – at least for logophiles – must remain untouched, even if the approach to its objects may be modified. In the first stage, the natural limits of Saussure's problematic are those of a highly specified corpus: the body of Saturnian poetry, largely of epigraphic origin. And it still only has to do with Saturnian verse as a *theoretical object*, namely a body of optimally concise simple rules; in fact, it is through the breach of this very 'simplicity' that the delirium will appear.

Saussure's research finally does exceed Saturnian verse, and, at the moment of its greatest extension, encompasses all ancient and modern poetry written in Latin; Saussure will even go so far as to seek answers to his questions from contemporary Latin poets. But at no moment does Saussure seek to transcend the regional horizon of a single tongue. The *individual language* (*la langue*) is at stake in his research, not *language in general* (*le langage*). And even less than with *the* language, what he works with are a few empirical rules that converge upon the system of the language to give that language a particular form. Logophilia is an empricism which takes language as it is, and only takes its structures *into account*, in order to transform it, through a definite practice, into an *artefact*. Saussure's notebooks, Brisset's texts, Roussel's fictions, Mallarmé's poems and Wolfson's narratives are all products of a craft, even if the goal of the practice is not the production of *objects* but the unveiling of a *truth*.

Contemporary paragrammatists err in citing Roussel, Brisset and Saussure as models. The latter work in the substance of the expression of concrete languages, and the laws which they discover or apply are specific, and limited to a strictly defined undertaking. Neither the thought nor the project of extrapolating their theories ever occurs to them; they never move in the direction of an analysis of the structure of their theories which would permit them to be formalized logically, beyond all empirical existence. Strictly speaking, there is never any movement on the part of the logophile to *apply* his theories: the laws which he unveils are in the strictest sense *immanent* to the objects which they govern. For them, there is but a single knowledge with two different modes of manifestation. Here we are at the antipodes of a movement such as OU.LI.PO., which on the contrary implements two different types of knowledge (linguistic on the one hand, logico-mathematical on the other) to produce new objects.

Despite occasional impulses to generalize, Saussure does not abstract a single law that would not immediately and uniquely refer back to the Latin texts. Likewise, Brisset in no way seeks to characterize an

unsuspected formal dimension of the signifier in general; on the contrary, it is when he is equal to such a task that the nature of his
undertaking begins to change: he passes from the *Logical Grammar* to
the *Science of God*, from the work of the grammarian seeking to
justify taxonomies, to the work of the prophet seeking to justify the
order of things human. His enterprise of abstraction and of rationaliza-
tion is rooted in a perfectly material *hic et nunc*. All of this is
symbolized by his having substituted for what could have become a
formal theory, something which is nothing other than a *history*. For
Roussel, who still possesses the dimension of the imaginary, the
production of history is replaced by that of *dictions*; but the place
of Roussel's novels within the organization of his delirium is
strictly homologous to that of the frog and the unwed-mother in
Brisset's. The same applies to the secret society of Latin poets for
Saussure.

Thus, however precise and alluring the 'formalization' of the anagram developed by Jean-Claude Lebensztejn in *La Fourche*, it opens
a combinatory which is without pertinence to the research of the logophiles, if their strategy concerning truth is considered. At most it
would permit a classification and a statistical analysis of their *procedures*: it could not in any case provide an inner perspective upon the
linguistic/desiring necessity which animates them, nor upon the heterogeneous logic which shapes the deliria in their specificity and their
generality.

Saussure thus characterizes the inferior limit of a vertigo born of
logophilic meditation: monoglossia. Limiting himself to a single language, he avoids confronting issues which could have led him, as in the
case of Brisset, to doubt the stability of laws that he otherwise considers beyond question – laws to which he confidently entrusts himself,
and which govern the organization and the history of languages. His
adventure only takes place within a specific zone of his knowledge,
even if the subsequent 'invention' of 'structural linguistics' can be considered as a by-product of the adventure of the anagrams.

But, even within such constraints, it must be recognized that Saussure did his utmost to explore as exhaustively as possible the domain
which he had laid out for himself. The extension and the comprehension
of the theory of the anagrams soon grew in an extraordinary manner;
this was the theoretical slope of what enlightenment may have been
for Saussure on the subjective level. It proceeds to a rapid annexation
of new phenomena – a veritable theoretical imperialism which submits

new territories to its laws, according to the multi-directional metonymy of desire. As the *Anti-Oedipus* states, this is 'axiomatization' conducted in the name of conquest and warfare (we have seen the use Saussure made of military metaphors: 'I have been advancing with heavy artillery . . . ,' etc.). To go from the very specific and highly localized problem of alliteration in the Saturnian verse, to that of a totalitarian vision which discovers the same phenomenon, the same law, in the entire Latin literary practice, both ancient and modern, is to cover an enormous distance. The *Blitzkreig* of desire, alone, permits it to be crossed. But the terrain is provided by the signifying materiality, which offers the reality of a texture, of a network whose laws are those of recurrence and regulated difference. The network of the signifier thus presents itself in a pure simultaneity: because nothing fissures the network, because the coupling operation is always possible, and because no signifier could be unmatched, its structure is exempt from time. Or, if time does exist, if something in languages represents its possibility, it would be *fiction*, the necessarily fictional history which shaped language in order to derive from its abstraction the empiricity of an enigmatic product: a network of texts. Beneath the immobility of the system, something is at work: an incessant Brownian movement of contrasts, resemblances, filiations initiated then eradicated, all both possible and impossible. This fiction which springs from the interrogation of the sign is 'historical' through and through, made up of plots, power struggles, conspiracies and repressions. This is a 'history' which Brisset and Roussel explore with obvious delectation, and one which Saussure clearly savours. From the mysterious relation between a language and the texts it made possible, the logophile derives a supplementary fiction which produces the mythic genealogy of the structure. It is here that the modern logophiles are closest to the classical semiosophists; of the latter, Sylvain Auroux wrote, for example: 'for the eighteenth century, language is an abstract structure whose elements are synchronically defined by their reciprocal relations, but . . . it is a panchronic reality, a monument for which history is not the locus of existence, but the trace of time within it.' What he says further of the concept of language for the same period defines with equal precision the mode of existence of language for the logophiles, including for Saussure in his work on the anagrams: 'a concept of language is constituted in the eighteenth century; it is not an abstract concept but what we might call a natural concept.'[27]

We shall return to the question of the significance of this encounter.

For the moment, it is enough to try to understand how language *exists* for our different logophiles. Roussel, for example, comes upon the same limits in his anagrammatic practice as did Saussure in his 'monoglossia'. It was no more for him than for Saussure a question of exceeding a fixed frame which functioned as *a priori* given, and imposing a single structure. The French language, in its capacity as a finite inventory of lexical components, serves as the material suited to Roussel's work. The corpus of words is a closed set for Roussel; whereas he may be able to constitute sub-sets susceptible to application within this corpus, the products of such operations remain subordinate to the transcendence of the dictionary. This may perhaps be what enables us to differentiate, in a typology, the discourse of the logophile from that of the creator of utopias: the exclusion of the neologism from the former versus its indispensable presence in the latter. For the logophile, the language (or languages) which forms the material substratum of his undertaking, functions systematically as a dead language. From this perspective, Fourier represents the exact opposite of someone like Brisset, despite the equally subversive political implications of *The Science of God* and *The New World in Love*. If it remains possible to speak of utopia in reference to the logophiles, its meaning must be restricted to the production of *fictions*, which are never proposed as a model for some future organization (including via a detour through a past or elsewhere); in the most extreme case it is but an hypothesis concerning real history; for all the others, it is only the imaginary in a pure state and without afterthought. Brisset and Saussure have to invent a counter-history and a censorship in order to explain the lack of traces; Mallarmé and Roussel are content with the 'other scene' as such.

It is against the background of such a determining difference that it is possible to understand the resemblances between the 'fictions' of men like Brisset, Roussel and Fourier, because they all result from the exploration of a *combinatory*. Roussel's fictions are the adventure of a discovery through the layers of language, across its every register, from scientific terminology to the different slangs, and through traditional novelistic vocabulary. Fourier, on the contrary, must go outside language in order to be able to imagine something *beyond* society. Wolfson's drama perhaps resides there, in the impossibility of *escape*, imprisoned as he is by that which antedates him. As for Saussure, the powers of archeology represent the absolute limits for any transformation of his corpus because, as a dead language, epigraphic discoveries alone would be equal to eventually enriching its dictionary. For Saussure, the combinatory presents an even more restricted field than it does for Brisset or Roussel, if only because of the simplicity of the rules organizing the course of signifiers in the texts. This has to do with a movement of reduction from the complex to the elementary, solidly inscribed in a scientific methodology validated by the tradition of linguistic studies. Ultimately, statistics should be able to take over from empirical research, in such a way as to determine in advance the 'discoveries' of the latter – Saussure gave it some thought. In this regard, he anticipated the gesture of Jean-Claude Lebensztejn; but he was sufficiently aware of its lack of pertinence to have been content with dreaming of it.

Without going so far as to produce a statistical and probabilistic interpretation of the anagrammatic operation such as it is found in Saussure and Roussel, it is possible to formally describe what we have called the 'combinatory', which represents the theory inherent to their practice. Or, more modestly, we could formulate in the following mann manner the base rule, which would then have to be analysed and specified: given a corpus, a set of transformational rules permits the generation of items which must themselves belong to the initial corpus; from the items of the corpus, another rule permits the generation of sequences of such items, which are also required to belong to the corpus. These rules are reversible, but each logophile uses them in only one direction; we shall see later what this implies. In more concrete terms, given that these rules apply only to the empirical material of the language, this would mean that words engender words, sentences, verses, narratives, etc. But the application of the rules can take place as well on sentences that have already been formed. The main point remains that the generative process must never overflow the limits of the given corpus: French returns to French, Latin to Latin, etc. Wolfson will be the *necessary* exception to the rule.

In so far as we can say that the practices of Saussure and of Roussel are strictly symmetrical to one another, the specific difference in their research must be sought in their relation to this common systematic core. Let us note first that, whereas Saussure starts with the intention of bringing the infinite back to the finite, Roussel takes pride, on the contrary, in opening up for future writers an inexhaustible mine, by exploiting the combinatory. In fact, Saussure starts with the *product* given in its completed historical existence, and strives to reach what he takes to be its seed and the mechanism of its production. He begins with *texts*, which he cannot alter, but whose every trait he assumes conceals the history of a production regulated by a calculable imperative; under no circumstances, for example, may a short vowel be substituted for a long vowel in the interest of coupling – Saussure only seldom invokes the alibi of 'licence'. Each phonetic and prosodic component is thus rigorously overdetermined, in such a way that the search for the hypogram is able to define with extreme precision the 'fork' out of which should appear the ordered sequence of phonemes which plays the role of 'kernel sentence' for the text which derives from it. The theory of the hypogram *supposes* the existence of the rules as an absolute; it excludes *a priori* the very possibility of the aleatory. By positing a proper noun as the sequence to be located, Saussure limits even further the eventual role of chance, in that the probability of discovering such a sequence beneath a text is considerably weaker than that of finding any other kind of word. It appears as though Saussure's undertaking consisted of attributing to Latin literature a rule which posits the practice of writing as nothing other than a treatment destined to reduce to zero the entropy characteristic of the formation of the strictly linguistic rules of natural languages. Writing consists of imposing an order upon that which knows none. Representing the taking-hold of language through the administration of an essentially hidden power, the anagram would be the logical agent of this regulation. Fundamentally, Saussure cannot resign himself to the existence of disorder in linguistic facts. His *Thesis* was already the product of such an impatience. The research on the anagrams is therefore nothing other than the daring short-cut of a thought which language resists; Saussure's desire is to get around an entire apparatus of rules that are difficult to formulate, to found, to justify. The anagrams represent a power-play which submits writing to the simplicity of a universal constraint. Here we find again the question of *power*, central throughout Cratylism, which Saussure proposes to solve in the form of the secret society of poets alluded to earlier. Only a conspiracy could impose upon language an order which would eliminate its fortuitousness – 'chance vanquished word by word,' said Mallarmé as well. This also permits us to understand the profound kinship between Saussure's desire and that of a certain contemporary Cratylism, intent upon 'remotivating' language through the literary operation – the studies of Roland Barthes and Gérard Genette on Proust could easily convince us of that fact. But Saussure is only engaged in a massive effort at *reduction*, through which he remains entirely faithful to his scientific character. For him, it is not a question of founding a theory of literature – although his studies on the legend of the Niebelungen do constitute a draft for such a theory, founded upon the same principles as the theory of the anagrams – and even less of *producing* literature. Restricting the research to Latin texts excludes *a priori* any overflow in this direction.

Roussel, for his part, takes hold of the same rules, but reverses the direction of the application. The kernel, word or sentence, is for him the point of departure, and not that of arrival; he produces a synthesis, he does not analyse a production. Saussure seeks words beneath verses he has not written, whereas Roussel begins with words he has chosen and from which he will derive narratives which he alone will control from beginning to end. Where Saussure, implicitly recognizing the creativity of the language as system, seeks to control it with rules which he assigns, and literally leave nothing to chance, Roussel incessantly defies chance by submitting the principle of reason incarnated by the rules to the pleasure principle that presides over productions of the imaginary. Through the application of the 'procedure', the disorder of language invests the closed field of representation where verisimilitude had reigned: the words disrupt the *doxa* of accepted notions about reality. The operation of language can embody the statue of the 'ilote' (Greek: *ilotes*, 'share') and the calves' lung rails, and go so far as to install them as disquieting simulacra on a theatrical stage, the prime locus of ambiguities of representation. Whence Roussel's 'unreasonable' insistence upon being staged at any cost. Through him, the anagrammatic practice discovers the language as *scene*, as a field saturated with the immanence of fiction. The avarice of Saussure's science gives way to the unbridled generosity of a discovery which finally permits poetry to be 'made by all' (according to the wish – produced by an error in reading – of Lautréamont). The promotion of entropy having been made possible through rules, Roussel discards these rules. Saussure's demanding rigour has no place in Roussel's practice. Each application of the rules Roussel sets for himself, on the contrary, explicitly foresees a role for the approximate and the arbitrary, either at the level of the selection of the kernel sentence, which could be the address of a tailor or a popular refrain, or at the level of the arrangement of the generated sequences. The products of an initial development can thus be distributed across an entire chapter or a whole book, without necessitating any further codification of their destination. The mechanism of overdetermination functions here in a manner very much like that found at work in the primary processes producing dreams.

Thus, for Roussel, the *fiction* is the end of any anagrammatic operation, whereas for Saussure it is but the remnant of that operation whose end is actually *science*. The stories of a secret society of poets are but a figuration of the need to fill a gap in the text of history. Roussel's narratives manifest, on the contrary, a profound indifference to the real, and transform reality in its entirety into an immense lacuna. For Roussel, what the real lacks is the imaginary. For Saussure, what is lacking from what he imagines, is a little reality. In this sense, if it is correct to say that Saussure's and Roussel's paragrammatic practices are founded on essentially identical principles, it must be specified that the resultant products will be inscribed in fundamentally different registers, the choice of which will manifest in each the trace of an entirely specific desire. From Saussure to Roussel there has been a change in the *codes* and *typologies* which present a conventional structure for accommodating the products of their operations. Saussure can only produce science, new chapters of knowledge, but they are entirely reinscribed in the language of the already-known: metrics, prosody, grammar; Roussel produces verse, drama, novels. Whether he is guided by science or fiction, the logophile remains, as we have noted, essentially conservative: no more than he would invent a neologism, a language, or a new society, would he invent a new science (it takes Brisset to go, at least apparently, a little beyond) or a new literary genre. He is satisfied with established knowledge and existing typologies. It is only Surrealist misunderstanding which sees a contradiction in Roussel's behaviour when he shows pride in his decorations and in his aristocratic and worldly ties. Saussure, the academician, remains an academician, if need be at the cost of his research on the anagrams. This is perhaps the consequence of 'monoglossia', which permits someone like Joyce or Artaud, or even Pound, to represent the possibility of a much vaster subversion than could ever derive from logophilia – which remains a theory of law and order, up through its accommodation of the approximate.

Within the systematic of logophilia, Roussel and Saussure remain inseparable, but their experience, though symmetrical and complementary, diverge. Together, they teach us that language is a Janus – or a Hermes. The roles of 'scriptor' (Roussel) or of 'decryptor' (Saussure) are but a contingent distribution along the endless eight[28] of the language as combinatory. Everything depends upon the focus of the subject who seeks to represent himself in his research. At the risk of losing himself, he ends up putting his own identity on the line, because language loses the ability to give back a reflection *of that subject,* as soon as it assumes the function of reflecting itself. As the phonemes, words, texts rearrange themselves, a subject is disseminated; but language remains endlessly confronted with itself, finding itself from one word to another, from one text to another, unable to escape from itself. Language has no 'depth'; there are no 'words beneath the words'. There is nothing but a surface, an infinite shimmering, the silvering of a mirror ceaselessly pulverized once a desire has traced its course upon it. Or else, if there is something 'beneath the words', it is a *narrative,* the resource of all fiction. Through his fictions, which he delivers from language, the logophilic subject brings himself into the world, a new world, which abruptly devours him, because it is himself *and* the Other. The formula for this logophilic self-devouring resides in the very name of Saussure – that is, if we follow the rules of his own practice: doesn't this name anagrammatize that of 'Saturn' (*Saturne*) and leave only, for one to emerge from the other, a remainder which poses their identity – 'Saussure Saturnus est'?

The limits inherent to the particular conditions of Saussure's and Roussel's 'deliria' thus prevent them from crossing a certain threshold, by constraining their desire to remain within a field defined by its closure. Their 'madness' remains within reason, and only produces effects in that zone in which their phantasy may be formalized. Neither science nor literature is greatly shaken: a split is produced in them which opens the space of an 'other scene', but which remains entirely isomorphous with what it fractures. Everything always comes back to linguistics or to the conventions of fiction. After Saussure, linguistic knowledge retains the ability to describe his work in the language or metalanguage which all linguists practise. The adventure of the anagrams can be read as the articulation of a theory, with its hypotheses and its conditions for validation or falsification; it can be judged and appreciated as any other discourse produced in the course of a particular history and which defines a field of knowledge recognized as such. Roussel gives us texts to read which we have always known how to classify as 'poetry', 'drama', or 'prose'. Considered independently of their source, texts such as *Impressions of Africa* or *Locus Solus* remain susceptible at all levels to readings based upon theories of the structural analysis of the narrative or any other semiotic theorization; these texts are constructed on the basis of characters and events; definite spatial and temporal relations order the adventures produced therein. Neither does anything prevent our studying Roussel in function of his reading of Jules Verne, nor our seeking to elucidate the constraints of an ideology (the positivist vision of the world, or the structures of the colonialist mentality, for example). The fact that this has not been done is due only to the historical contingency of our being able to read *How I Wrote Some of My Books*. And yet it should be done, because what interested Roussel himself was not so much his 'procedure' as the texts which could result from it, and which he conceived of as proof of his desire to be nothing but a 'writer of the imagination'. Roussel's texts are *also* cultural objects offered up to a certain mode of symbolic consumption that 'madness' has nothing to do with, because there it cannot be *seen*.

What Brisset and Wolfson propose for us is an altogether different matter. The formal limits of established typologies do not concern them in the least, and hold no determining pertinence or *power* of reinscription for them. Addressing readers, they are not satisfied with the normalized encoding of the receiver, which is one of the conventions founding literature or science as such. He whom they interpellate is not the subject of a standardized practice of the sign; they do not propose to complete for their reader the gesture of a dialectic which they would have inaugurated for the sole purpose of his conferring upon it the marker of reality that would confirm its meaning. They address a subject *like themselves*, a subject of the sign and of desire, and not one *represented* by the sign. Their struggle is that of a truth seeking to bring all truth to the light of day – even if one considers that the subject to whom they address this pathetic interpellation is none other than themselves: Wolfson uncertain of his being, Brisset dissolved in the light of Being. This emphatically underscores the distance separating an ardent practice which is, none the less, free of any irreversible urgency, from a delirium that has become irrepressible through desire's having entirely disclosed and become taken with itself, and that is striving to uphold itself by speaking solely in its own name. This distance is the very one which distinguishes what we have called 'monoglossia' from *panglossia*.

In the words of Gilles Deleuze in his presentation of *The Schizo and Languages*, Wolfson's goal is to 'reunite all foreign languages into a continuous idiom'.[29] The fundamental imperative of Wolfson's labour, its necessity and its fatality, literally consists of redoing what Babel

57

undid; the unity of the human idiom, beyond the structures which
make each language an isolated system. For Wolfson, a language is not
a repertory of words or sequence of phonemes, in which the phoneme
represents the passageway for communication from one language to
another – albeit at the price of an occasional forcing. In a sense, lexical
inventories are but a convenience which facilitates Wolfson's circulation
from one language to another – or rather, from *one* language to all the
others. For this 'idiom', whose vocabulary he aims to constitute as a
single list through which he could circulate without being arrested for
more than an instant by the viscosity of the signifier, is in actuality
composed of *all languages but one*: English. At the heart of this zone
of free linguistic exchange, there is a whirling hollow of perdition,
which he must flee. It is a question of life and death. Wolfson's entire
effort consists of endlessly repeating the gesture which sets him on a
centrifugal trajectory; he must in a sense become a satellite which
orbits at the greatest possible distance from English – his maternal
tongue, the language of his mother which destroys him. But relentlessly, the gravity which forms the core of his being, a kind of impersonal
will which annuls his own, draws him anew to the unbearable centre
where he dies. The entire technique perfected by Wolfson thus consists above all of dividing languages into two groups, in such a way
that a frontier separates the two groups and provides a surface where
he can circulate perilously. His journey, however, is not a journey
across languages *in general*: his problem is not to cross from just any
language to just any other; he must always cross from English to any
language in the group of foreign languages – the only prerequisite being
rapidity. Like a smuggler or a poacher, he will seek out open passage-
ways that he can rely upon to pass to the other side, into friendly
territory. Ultimately, what he seeks to perfect and memorize is a
dictionary of available and reliable pathways. Unlike that of the Cratylists and etymologists of the eighteenth century, Wolfson's work
therefore has no historical dimension; for him, Babel does not mark
the limit between a before and an after, but, on the contrary, the
impalpable frontier between a here and a there, between danger and
safety, between life and death. For him, all time is condensed in that
instant when he escapes, in that minute delay that threatens him without respite, and that is the exact opposite of historical time unfurled.
It takes but a second for English to catch up with him, to penetrate
his ears and his body, to lacerate him with its torments.

If rapidity is a vital requirement for the defence mechanism perfected by Wolfson to operate in complete safety, there are nevertheless a certain number of intrinsic formal conditions which slow down its application. These conditions are in fact veritable *rules* which he must rigorously respect, lest he stray. The first rule defines his obligation, when seeking a passageway, to maximally preserve the characteristics of the phonic signifiers of the English words he must transform. The substituted sounds must be as close as possible to the original ones. But that is not all; he could conceivably be satisfied, like Roussel in a sense, with finding, in a German, Russian, Hebrew or French word, the same sounds but in a different order, or present more than once in the same word. Not in the least: the entire phonematic sequence must remain intact, once it has been transposed from the source word to the target word. As with Saussure, nothing must linger, no stray remnant, no signifier drifting to one side of the frontier or the other. A single unmatched signifier would be invested with all the suffering he seeks to elude, and there would be no proportional diminution of its pangs. The law of couplings must discover perfectly isomorphous series, as infinitely close to each other as possible. No space may subsist between them save that reserved for what Deleuze calls elsewhere *the object x*, the 'sombre resonator': the locus of the subject himself in his status of lacuna permitting the juncture of languages. These first two rules are completed by a third which compounds Wolfson's suffering by complicating the means he gives himself to escape it, and also functions as the motor for what he himself calls his 'mania': not only must he conserve the structure of the signifier in its entirety, he also requires of his system that the signified in turn pass, without remainder or surplus, from one side of the frontier of Babel to the other. The task is impossible: the maximal conservation of the signifier *and* the signified is finally nothing other than Wolfson's auto-imposition of a *double bind* (to use Bateson's terminology) which reproduces the fundamental structure of his psychosis. The combat he must wage in the fraction of a second it takes for an English word to penetrate his body takes on the dimension of an impossible epic: a struggle lost in advance against the work of entropy, inherent to any operation of translation or transcoding. Wolfson imposes upon himself a condition which implies, from the outset and prior to any effort, that he has no chance of ever successfully respecting it. Suffering is inevitable; at most he can succeed in attenuating it, by resigning himself to the permanent tension required to remain alert, and to the infinite work of refining his dictionary of linguistic sanctuaries. A martyr of translation,

Wolfson sacrifices his intelligence and his body to the reconstruction of Babel.

We will note here that Wolfson, like Brisset and Roussel, has no thought of producing a new language, for which he would set codes, and which would compensate for the insufficiencies of each language which has not provided signified and signifying series totally isomorphous to those of English. By studying an increasing number of languages, Wolfson, like the poet according to Mallarmé, strives to 'remunerate the deficiencies of languages'. This is an interminable undertaking that a personal Esperanto could have greatly simplified, had the rationality of an economic calculation been able to find a place in that which recognizes only the law of desire, whose despotism cannot be repelled. Like Mallarmé, Saussure, and Roussel, Wolfson comes face to face with something like a transcendence, an enigmatic being which effects the collusion of a desire and a form. This elusive phantom, some aspect of which escapes from every grasp, whether it be that of science, literature, or whatever, is the *sign*. The absolute horizon of pleasure and suffering, of being and knowledge. Wolfson cannot tolerate the idea of splitting the sign, and isolating the signifier from the signified. The technique of universal translatability which he institutes from one language to all the others seeks only to preserve the integrity of the *meaning*, on condition that it be free to migrate, to circulate among all languages without coming up against the frontiers of a system which would arrest its flux, on condition that it be able to reterritorialize or expatriate itself at will. This promotes an incessant motility agitating from within the paradoxical content of a membrane, which makes languages a coalescence of sounds and meanings struggling against chance. The French in which Wolfson finally tells his story constitutes a makeshift solution, the stasis of a respite in the depths of a temporary refuge to which he episodically manages to withdraw. In no sense is it a metalanguage with which the manipulator would put an end to the manipulations which affect him. There is no more a place in Wolfson's adventure for a metalanguage, than there is for any Esperanto – thereby verifying Lacan's formula. Language remains for him an empirical continuum; the territory cannot be divided so as to permit the emergence of a mastery, nor is there any possibility of a reprieve in which the subject would no longer be in question, in which the interrogation which continually calls him into question would lose its impact. In other words, for Wolfson, there is no *science*. The linguistics which he uses functions at best as a methodology, a technique for reinforcing his resistances. Within the economy of his suffering, linguistics is of value to him only because it permits an analysis of the *sign*. For, in order to maintain the constructive bond of the sign which, as we have seen, is of vital importance to Wolfson, he must first and even in spite of himself undo it. He must isolate the signifying agent, analyse it, and dismember it. Only then can he substitute for it another signifying whole that will link up with the signified which has been set aside, and form, on the other side of the frontier, a new sign which inhabits another territory, and is therefore safe. The signifier must lose its signified in order for the subject to escape from it again. The twin faces of the sign are orphans, until the crossing of the frontier of langages symbolizes that of the bar which separates them to better unite them. Ever since the Saussure of structural linguistics, Wolfson's impossible adventure sums up the pathos of the sign. The bar separates and unifies; the orphan becomes so only to better find its father; in spite of everything, the new sign still alludes to the old. At the figurative level, the bond of the signifier to the signified is thus a veritable umbilical cord (which then takes on a paternal as well as maternal value); for Wolfson, it is a symbol of the one he strives to sever or to deny yet which none the less continues to tie him to his mother, to his maternal tongue – even in the means he adopts to escape them.

Wolfson emblematizes the particular work of logophilia: an unconscious conflict, a network of desire painfully bound, mobilize the defences of a subject by exposing him to his own failure-to-be (*manque-à-être*), constrain him to turn upon himself that Medusa's gaze in which he reads the unbearability of castration; this reveals the fragility of the symbolic and the exhaustion of the reflective. It is thus at the heart of the symbolic, with its materials and its laws, that something will seek to reconstruct itself behind the entrenchment of negation. The subject deprived of a locus – whether in anguish or in ecstasy – thus inhabits that which contains the very possibility of a locus, of time, of speech: language itself, worked upon by knowledge and practices. The conflict becomes a semiotic compromise, the search for an order which would be the conquest of a peace without surprise – *pax semiotica*, which assures, depending upon the inclination of each, rest or glory, survival or apotheosis. Wolfson himself only remains within meaning and sociality at the cost of an immense effort at semiotic reorganization, a belabouring of languages. By setting up his meticulously programmed apparatus for instantaneous decoding-encoding, he wrests from the hold of the entropy which undoes him something like a simulacrum which adequately stands in for him: this 'schizophrenic' of his narrative who condenses all his ability and will to survive. His transformative activity therefore does not proceed fortuitously in accordance with some exploded 'genotext', but rather manoeuvres to produce a repertory of precise movements that will globally constitute a strategy, by putting at his disposal a selection of possible parries in case of immediate danger. Each entrance to his permanent lexicon is a weapon of warfare – a formulaic, magical ritual which 'linguistics' only superficially naturalizes. Through the institution of a surveillance covering all horizons, Wolfson's paragrammatism is a work of *saturation*, but it is also a patient and methodical work of *suturation* which aims to reduce the gap through which anguish and danger can always return and always threaten. Like Mallarmé's Nothingness, Saussure's lost poet, the whole of Roussel's narratives, such a gap is beyond reach because it is also the separation from the mother, castration or the splitting of the subject in the symbolic, the articulation of language or the distinction between the signifier and signified. Saturation and suturation: therein lies all the research of Cratylism, as does that of the remotivation of work within literature, within poetry, so too does that of the logophile questioning the sign through its subject, as does finally that of metaphysics applying itself to arrest the drifts that overflow Being, God, History. It is a tireless attempt to relieve the very work of *difference* in bodies, subjects, knowledge, texts and in worlds.

Wolfson, like Pascal, as well as any man, carries his abyss within him, and is at each moment threatened with disappearing into it and becoming pure anguish in the adventure of an irreversible alienation. This abyss is the sign; force it, and the thread which assures us of the real and guarantees us our bodies, distends. And this is also why Wolfson must always plug his ears, to protect them from linguistic aggression. These thresholds contain the truth of the subject, for whom the difference between full and empty is slight, fragile; his is a cavernous body which a phoneme fraying a path could pierce, a *tympan* whose resonances Derrida let us hear. Schreber and Brisset's 'voices' are but the clamour awakened in the depths of this threshold by the discovery of the signifier; for Wolfson, it is the very voice of his mother which speaks within him and which he wants to expel. For Saussure, as for Roussel, it is the inspiration which dictates the anagrams and the narratives. But, as with Mallarmé, the question of the body is not limited to listening to its echoes: it is a suffering, eradicable materiality. Wolfson must endlessly protect its unity from the menace of a split – such as Mallarmé's during his journey to Idumaea – that would disseminate and destroy him; to this end, he gluts himself on food to the point of nausea, in order to create a full body upon which the flux can slide. As with Sartre nausea is finally a proof of being for Wolfson. What is at stake in the paragrammatic principle, the real scope of panglossia, the end of the regulated anaphoric references, is not simply the hidden depth of language for Wolfson; it is himself. To varying degrees, this will remain true for all logophiles who are not simply sophists of the sign.

Brisset, however, knows nothing of that constantly threatened trembling which constitutes the fragility of the logophile. Or rather, he understood it so well that he knew how to go beyond it; yet, unlike Wolfson, his is not a laborious flight. Brisset, on the contrary, deliberately throws himself into the abyss which he has discovered, and it is there that he can find his salvation. He too faces words that suddenly split, signs that come undone, meanings that capsize. But, instead of opening on to a void, they open like a series of successive doors which show Brisset the path to a Sky. Behind the sign, there is a god. The wreck of signs no longer ushers in an anguish but an ecstasy. Mallarmé had known something like this for a time, but he had been unable to sustain it: the ruin of the sign had become his own. In facilitating his recovery, 'science' had only left him an ambiguous memory: Hérodiade. Brisset's Hérodiade is God. The word which had painfully resonated at the threshold of the body for Wolfson, emerges from the depths of Brisset's being, and is inhabited by its divine host. The voices which he hears become his own. His entire body becomes the spokesman for the truth which is his to broadcast: Brisset becomes an angel of the Apocalypse whose proclamation he trumpets forth with his voice. Brisset has become Word, host of God. Blended in with this demanding and benevolent Other, he participates in its generous and fruitful omnipotence. But this does not come to him free of requirements: Brisset has not simply won a paradise that would assure him of rest. An anxiety subsists, that is entirely invested in a research which is not so much that of hidden discourses as it is that of the *other*: he is bound to spread his knowledge, to extend it to other men so that they may know what narratives are concealed within the generosity and fecundity of the Word. This makes Brisset a *prophet*, the herald of a new regime of signs, which had always been waiting within words that all had believed mute, and which only needed a human speech to become animated.

Owing to the privilege of his mission, Brisset's sacred horror is discovered in the very hollow of the words he thought belonged to him:
two voices speak from the same throat. For him, everything takes
place as if human language were but a disguised, misunderstood glossolalia: everyone 'speaks in tongues', at every instant; whereas it may
have taken the experience of an enlightenment to understand it, all
its benefits may be derived through simple reason. The prophetic
experience is thus broken down for Brisset into two separate moments:
the first is that of enlightenment which is the enigmatic privilege of a
single person, the second is that of the rational exploitation of the discovered truth. Following the mystical experience, linguistic practice
fills in for its eradication. The ecstasy can be dispensed with. This is
all, naturally, underpinned at the figural level by the topos of Christ:
it only takes one person to announce the truth; once this has been
done, the good word is within anyone's reach – all it takes is good will.
In the most rational sense, Brisset presents himself as an evangelist.

Nevertheless, the agency of rationality holds a preponderant place
in the configuration of his experience. The knowledge with which
Brisset started out does not disappear beneath his belief; on the contrary, he applies that knowledge which, to a certain extent, makes the
belief possible. Predictably, that knowledge is once again linguistics. In
an initial phase, his delirium derives from the midst of the classical
episteme, structural and rationalist, and is applied to the examination
of linguistic problems. Like the Saussure of the anagrams, Brisset
strives to resolve a problem; perhaps impatient, he finds, like Saussure,
a short-cut that will simplify everything.

The problem which concerns him throughout the first part of his
logophilic career is relatively simple: how do you rationalize the teaching of the French language? The undertaking does not fail to engage
a powerful ambition, but it is nevertheless quite ordinary. In a period
which witnessed the birth of compulsory schooling, nothing could be
more legitimate than this pedagogic aspiration – a highly common sort
of paranoia which was wholly acclimatized to the culture. The first
form of Brisset's delirium remains perfectly logical and strictly preoccupied with the solution of a taxonomic problem. On the basis of
accepted knowledge, Brisset strives to reorganize the givens of the language, in the simple hope of introducing a more convincing order to the
tableaux which present the facts of the language, and thereby inducing
efficacious rules. Brisset does not infringe upon language: he neither
revises the models which permit the classification of morphological

facts, nor proposes new hypotheses which would lead to a revision of the history of the language. He does not stray from his role as a grammarian. On the contrary, he is careful to respect traditional forms of knowledge, including those with an early Saussurian resonance (associated with the notion of structural grammar); the proof is in a declaration such as the following one: 'One can no more modify a language in one of its parts than a mathematical relation in one of its numbers.'[30]

It is true that here Saussure no doubt plays the role of a screen memory, and that we must seek to understand this conception uttered by Brisset as a function of more distant antecedents – and not only those of Philology but also and especially those which formed a part of the classical *episteme*: Cuvier's brand of structuralism. Brisset no doubt returned to Port Royal and to the *General Grammar* before Saussure. In fact, the title of his principal linguistic work acknowledges the debt: *The Logical Grammar*. It is as if Brisset had successfully blended Grammar and Logic in order to finally create that portmanteau science which others before him had dreamed of, beginning with Leibniz and his project of a universal characteristic. Yet, in the first phase of his research, he restricts himself to monoglossia, and at no point becomes involved in inventing his own Esperanto. Like all the other logophiles, Brisset will only be able to find universality in what already exists. In spite of his 'logical' requirement, his work remains essentially founded upon an insurmountable empiricism, and attached to a research which remains flush with a chaos of the language that he is only concerned with ordering. When he achieves a measure of success, by establishing paradigms for the formal (morphological) relations which define configurations that strictly exist synchronically in the language, he anticipates what Saussure (second epoch) will bring. He begins to resemble the Saussure of the anagrams, however, when, from what he considers the success of his efforts at classification, there suddenly appears the possibility of a new and unknown knowledge, which has announced itself in the mode of a revelation. Brisset suddenly sees before his eyes the unveiled possibility of an entirely hidden history: 'The Word, which is God, has conserved within its folds the history of the human species from the first day; and in each idiom, the history of each people, with a certainty, an irrefutability which will confound the simple and the wise.'[31]

After all, Brisset has done no more here than take literally what the Christian tradition has taught him: God is the Verb. Literally, in the sense that, for him, there could be no difference between this notion of 'Verb' and that which simply designates language. Through an audacious ellipsis, language is converted into *the individual tongue*: the Word is the tongue. No place is left for metaphorization, which would permit the introduction of that essential distance between words through which figuration becomes possible; the detour, rhetoric, in short, can find no place in the economy of a regime of the sign which does not allow for any floating of the signified. Brisset's tongue functions as an antihermeneutic, a code constantly maintained at degree zero. Every disorder is *a priori* excluded, as could be expected from Brisset's victory over the entropy, which had appeared to be constitutive of any undertaking designed to put a grammar in order. Every meaning will always be literal for him – which is a perfectly logical fulfilment of the classical requirement which informs Brisset, and according to which the metaphor could only be an ornament, a suspect and somewhat superfluous luxury which is furthermore supervised by the rhetorician devoted to classifying its genres and species. Brisset thus appears as a distant cousin of du Marsais. The hypothesis of an *a priori* order of language unequivocally inscribes Brisset in the Cratylist lineage. His own effort will consist of remotivating the language, *the entire language*, through a gesture which we have already analysed in relation to Saussure.

Yet, in telling us further that the Word 'has conserved in its folds the history of the human species, from the first day', Brisset traverses another period of the history of science, where he comes upon one of the fundamental convictions of many of the 'semiosophists' of the eighteenth century. Etymology, before becoming a science (but let us recall the ambiguity of Saussure's position before the 'miracles' of popular etymology), remains something like a divination, which asks a very specific question: where does man come from? Before becoming a science of the history of language, etymology is a science of the history of man. The entire thematic and problematic of the original language are nourished in the eighteenth century by this preponderant concern. What was the first language? How did the first men live? How was society formed? How did the original language become bastardized to the point of producing the numerous dialects that we know today? In his own way, Brisset strives to answer these questions, and the solutions which he provides differ very little from those which the literati of the preceding century had passionately discussed. As Sylvain Auroux states in the work cited earlier, 'the problem of the origin of

languages was in the eighteenth century the place where reflection
sought to envision heterogeneous problems in a unitary fashion.'[32]
Brisset's hypothesis, which evidently sets God at the origin of everything, is no more 'mad' than, for example, that of Poisinet de Sivry,
for whom the original language could only have been Celtic, because
there were discernible traces in numerous languages of Celtic words
connected with fire and heat – and this because, according to his
theory, meetings around a primordial fire would have led the Celts
to constitute the first human society. Viewed from this angle, current
languages would certainly contain a literal memory of their history.
The difference, of course, remains that this author did not extract
from his hypothesis, as did Brisset, the *detail* of this history. Furthermore, the language which he situates at the origin is unique, in
accordance with the logic of the research conducted by that epoch;
Brisset, however, does not pose the problem of this single language.
For him, there was no Babel; each language has always existed as it
now does; there is no unity between them except at the level of the
principle which provides each with the same law for situating its relation to the history of the people who spoke, and perhaps still speak
it. Brisset is therefore closer to Condillac and Rousseau, for whom there
was not *one* but *several* first languages. This would not alter the fact
that man has always been the same, and that his mode of acquiring
language has always been identical, regardless of the diversity of the
first languages. At the latter level, Brisset's theory on the historical
memory of languages represents only the 'stronger' form of a conception that was common in the eighteenth century, though more hesitant
as to detail. For Condillac, the first human sounds imitated the sounds
produced by objects: this was the 'language of action'; for de Brosses
as well, language results from the reaction of man to his environment,
etc. In a certain sense, it could be said that, if Brisset is prone to a particular type of madness, it is situated first at the level of epistemology,
because he basically accepts *at the same time* all existing theories: the
one according to which man created language before creating societies;
the one which claims the opposite; the more orthodox one which sees
God as having equipped man with language and socialized him, prior
to any history. Brisset 'crushes' any history which is not purely and
simply the history of man: this history is found inscribed *in* languages,
but languages, *as such*, have no history.

The very natural conclusion which Brisset draws from his premises
is that neither Latin nor Sanskrit ever existed these languages can only

be purely artificial because they no longer exist. There were no peoples to support them; in particular, the Romans therefore could only have spoken *Italian* – the language, still according to Brisset, in which the *Sermons of Strasbourg* were written, if one allows for slight differences of nuance. In refusing to acknowledge the filiation of Latin and French, Brisset actually rejoins his predecessors: neither Poisinet de Sivry, Crandval, nor 'B.E.R.M.' (the author of the article 'language' in the *Encyclopédie*) accepts Latin as being at the origin of French. Of course, they generally substitute one, or several other languages for Latin, and thus retain the notion of a temporality proper to the development of languages. This, Brisset does not do: for him, time did not take place. This is the very order which one discovers in each language which, as system, thereby designates its own origin. History is no more than the past anterior of the structure; we might say the history *alongside* the structure. But there is a contradiction here which Brisset does not seem to realize: on the one hand he tells us that each natural language, 'each idiom', has conserved 'the history of each people'; but, on the other, what he tells us, and furthermore derives from an analysis of French, is the only history of the 'ancestors of man'. This history is therefore the history of what was *before* history. Not satisfied to reach back to the time of Babel, Brisset reaches back to what preceded man himself. It is only at this level that the origin coincides with language, and that the origin is *always already linguistic*. Thus, language is no longer a simple supplement to the voiceless presence of an event: event and language are one, every event begs a word, and the language as a whole is the very voice of this network of events in which the origin is formed. The language does not speak of origins; the origin speaks through it. All it takes is to open the *words* for an entire lost memory, which never gave rise to *discourse*, to re-emerge intact. The discourse, the text were subsequently able to become the reflections of events on the basis of the origin. But this was a matter of *writing*; it is only in *speech* that the original and the copy were able to blend:[33]

> We are therefore going to rediscover the terrestrial paradise, the times when beasts and men spoke together: we will see the gods climb to the sky and descend to earth. The fabled dragons will be reborn before our eyes, and we will feel the fright of our ancestors. All this is written in the language.

This is a radical logocentrism for which the exclusion of writing

takes the form of its reintegration into the very process of the formation of speech. The logophile, tireless writer, only recognizes the right
of speech to have memory. The Mallarmé of the *Mots anglais* also only
recognized meaning in phonemes; the voice was the node of Wolfson's
suffering and his resistance; in applying his procedure, Roussel was only
concerned with the series formed by sounds; Saussure had to suppose
an *oral* transmission of the secret of composition he wanted to have
discovered, and even his meditation on writing, in the anagrams notebooks, submitted the *Stab* (origin of graphism) to the necessities of
a calculation which only concerned phonemes. Yet, for each of them,
writing, whether subjected to repression or negation, re-emerges everywhere, and conquers the role of indispensable medium for the
exposition of theses which deny it. For them as well, the contradiction
of the Occident shapes in depth every practice and every theory.

Once history has been evacuated – the one concerning what follows
the origin – everything is possible, and it is clear that Brisset takes particular delight in announcing that everything will at last be revealed to
us. Having annulled the repression, the phantasy can blossom in its
absence. For Brisset, this is the only history which matters: true *fiction*,
literal myth. The fiction (the history of the ancestors of man) can
henceforth develop freely, on the basis of a focused reading of the
language. Once he has crossed to the other side of the origin, Brisset
will no longer recall the differences which he recognized between
languages and which should have permitted his distinguishing the
histor*ies* of particular peoples. All languages now designate for him
the same history, and he will be content to snatch up one word or
another, depending upon the urgency of his vision. Brisset henceforth
approaches languages as an open book, and does no more than *translate* the words of the various languages into this event-language in which
the figure of man is born. Panglossia settles in at full strength. To the
extent that he situates his entire study at a register which does not take
into account the particular system of each natural language (like Wolfson or Mallarmé: *syntax* does not exist, which poses an irreducible
difference; let us note that it is precisely upon syntax that Mallarmé,
in an admittedly conservative move, later relies), the history discovered
by Brisset can only transcend the differences between the languages,
and between the communities which made them. To forget syntax in
order to promote letter-sounds, letter-meanings, is automatically to
erase what we recognize as real history, and to substitute a universal
history. In this respect, Brisset is aligned with the great, epic visionaries

of the eighteenth century, who wrote immense didactic poems concerning the original idiom of man – obsessed with Man, forgetful of men.
Logophilia and fiction commune in a passion for the origin. Things
were no different for the 'scientific' eighteenth century; this was what
led Bopp 'to want to find terminations of the root *es*, 'to be', the
"abstract" verb, the original "substantive" verb'.[34] This was also the
case for de Piis, Court de Gébelin or even for Fabre d'Olivet: in the
same spirit, Brisset wrote:[35]

> By examining the endings of the future infinitive of verbs
> in Romance languages: *are, ar, er, ere, ir, ire, aire, ore, oire,*
> *ure, urre, re* etc., we were struck by their analogy, and con-
> cluded that this ending had a common origin; that this
> origin could only be logical, and that it was the Latin verb
> *ire* (to go) in different forms.

Unfortunately for Brisset, science had changed sides in the course of
a century; the respected paradigms had come undone, and what could
have legitimately passed one hundred years earlier for a rational speculation is greeted as a phantasmagoria at the point when historical
linguistics and comparative grammar have already lived their triumph;
the 'second' Saussure is preparing to launch yet another revolution. But
Brisset or something within him is unaware of this, and his madness is
only the consequence of the cunning of epistemology. At the moment
when the 'structure' is about to appear, Brisset, like Bopp, is still
questioning the origin:[36]

> *I*, this was the first human utterance. It is the universal cry,
> the first human cry emitted by the child as it comes into
> the world . . . . Whatever modifications it is made to undergo
> in forming the language, we will always find *i*, whether be-
> neath another intonation, whether preceded or followed by a
> liaison whose sound will accompany it and that we call con-
> sonant.

The detour through the origin permits the triumph of panglossia;
and it matters little to Brisset that he has declared Latin an artificial
language: it is in Latin that he will seek the confirmation of his vision
and the absolute origin of all language. Everything takes place as if
the structure of Brisset's research had adopted a conformation perfectly
isomorphous to that of his delirium: the origin transcends the derivative

differences; the truth of each partial field matters less than the central thesis. The same proposition could therefore be true or false, depending upon its tactical value in a given strategy. Latin must not exist if Brisset wishes his political thesis to be convincing; it must exist if there is to be a coherent vision of phylogenesis. The linguist and the prophet do not necessarily have the same things at stake: each element of empirical analysis can be interpreted on both planes at the same time. In such circumstances, the case of the *I* is doubtless for Brisset the desired argument, because this *I* is doubly original: at the origin of all other phonic combinations, and at the origin of man as speech and as history. 'Ontology' and 'linguistics' start here from the same point, and it is their original community which permits founding the singleness of their double discourse; it is because there was this primordial, two-sided *I* that Brisset could listen to the language and translate it word by word as a history of man. In general terms, logophilia is sustained by this splitting of the origin. Mallarmé sought the point at which sound and meaning had yet to become distinguishable; for Wolfson, the split was the bottomless pit which had to be filled in, at the level of sequences that had to be absolutely differentiated while remaining perfectly identical; Roussel's time was spent discerning, beneath a word or sentence, the other series which divided it from within; and Saussure himself does likewise when he suspects the existence, beneath each phoneme, of another, rigorously identical phoneme, yet which belongs to an entirely different word. For the logophile, there is never a pure, unique, and absolute origin; every beginning is always already divided. And, whereas their entire undertaking aims to suture the fault which splits the origin, their texts can only be inscribed in the gap which they explore while proclaiming that it does not exist. This doubling of the origin corrupts the core and thwarts its thrust. Derrida's analysis of Husserl in *Speech and Phenomena* would thus also constitute the best possible commentary upon logophilia.

The necessity for universality thus takes form within the anxiety of the origin. Because every sound, and even the first of all, is already double, all languages must communicate with each other in order to restore the unity that was lost at the origin. Panglossia is inseparable from the discovery of the origin, and thus designates the natural empirical field for the exploration to be conducted: 'This theory applies not only to Spanish and Italian, but to Greek, Arabic, German and probably to all languages.'[37]

Here we again come upon what Deleuze had noted with regard to

71

Wolfson: all languages form but a single continuous idiom, and the
discourse of truth about man passes through glossolalia, but instituted
by and under the cloak of science. Throughout the many languages
of men, it is Man as such who tells his history. From God to the Word,
from the Word to Man, from Man to Brisset, the chain is continuous:
everything which speaks, speaks 'in tongues'. Brisset's evangelism is
a fundamentalism owing to its universal combinatory; the Word as
a continuous idiom, woven with the diversity of languages, raises
the historico-semantic differences between all languages. Synchrony
and diachrony can be collapsed against one another to form a single
reality, a unique dimension which divides man's existence to the
extent that he is a speaking being, and from before the beginnings
of his history. As we stated, Brisset does not explain why events
are not memorized in the Word from the moment at which man is
definitively formed and becomes separated from his antehistorical
origins; it is because language exists for him – although this is never
said – as speech and as writing. As speech, it is a true, material,
immediately figurative memory; as writing, it is a bad memory, a
derived reflection, a simple discursive instrumentality; not immediate,
deferred, it is a dead memory. For Brisset, *sound* alone recalls the
scenes that were believed forgotten and brings to life the phantasy
as an enlightenment.

The consequences of the panglossic theory upon the structure of
the linguistic knowledge which guarantees it are important. There is
no more linguistic system. In the *Logical Grammar* a word existed at
the intersection of several paradigms, in the field of several rules; their
network defined the specificity of the language in its difference from
all others. Now, with the *Science of God*, the system no longer has
either a centre or a periphery, neither exterior nor interior: all languages enjoy an absolute contemporaneity in the synthesis of the
origin, in such a way that the *meaning* can no longer derive from the
particular rules of one system or another, which distribute the relations between signifiers and signifieds according to an order which is
each time specific. Where, then, will Brisset be able to localize meaning?
What will be the locus of its emergence? In order to be able to situate
it, one must dispose of a stable means of positing the relation of meaning to the idiom which transcends the individual differences held to be
inessential. This means is the same one which Mallarmé was already
using – meaning will only be accessorily linked to words and lexemes
As a fundamental kinship between all the sounds of all the languages

is already supposed (Saussurian phonology does not yet exist), the
solution is right at hand:[38]

> Every syllable which enters into the formation of a word con-
> tains at least one particular idea. In a language, in order to find
> this idea, one must gather as many words as possible in which
> this syllable is found, and look for the expression most suited
> to the greatest number of cases.

This was componential analysis before the fact, and the theory of
Brisset or of Mallarmé is the true ancestor of the theory of semic
analysis. From there, an entire chain is reconstituted, stretching from
the linguists of the eighteenth century, to Mallarmé, to Brisset, and up
to Greimas or Pottier.

On the linguistic plane, Brisset's theory also presents another characteristic which relates it to the work of Schlegel, Bopp, and especially
Humboldt. At this level, the fantasy, ideology and science all become
completely indissociable. Having established as the goal of his work the
research for the expression which could yield a kind of semantic largest
common denominator, Brisset goes on to state:[39]

> If this expression illuminates each word with a new light, it
> is just; it is perfect if it receives an analogous value in properly
> Germanic words, and must, with mathematical certitude,
> receive the same value in the idioms of India. For this study,
> all languages and dialects, whatever they may be, must be
> made available. *But it is especially in the pronunciation of
> uncultivated languages or patois that nature may best be
> grasped.*

The promotion of 'patois' is surely a Romantic trait, in its desire to
hear the true nature of the people spoken. But, on the other hand, we
have already seen that Brisset's exclusion of Latin as a natural language
was largely based upon a classical precedent, which allowed legitimate
doubts to be cast upon the filiation from Latin to French. The priori-
ties here are difficult to establish. Within his system, is it an ideologically-
determined interest in popular languages which accounts for the
exclusion of Latin and Sanskrit from the history of natural languages?
Or is it the opposite? Given the investment of desire manifest in the
treatment of this question in Brisset's texts, we believe that ideology

did in this instance play the role of a catalyst, if not that of an initiator; for him, in fact, Latin and Sanskrit became entirely *artificial* languages, invented by a dominating caste to preserve and perpetuate its domination of an exploited mass. What had clearly euphoric connotations for Saussure (the freemasonry of poets) takes on a perfectly evident dimension of social and political claims with Brisset. At this point something completely different from a logophilic perspective is introduced to the logic of Brisset's delirium. Violence and power suddenly appear as profoundly intertwined, woven into the very course of speech. Throughout this discourse, the echoes of a revolt can be heard; its origin is unknown but it is invested with insistence in a political vision. Brisset thereby belies the alleged neutrality of science. The class struggle in theory is there in its entirety; against the aristocratic conceptions of the history of languages, Brisset takes a stand for a theory designed to reveal the pre-eminence of the people. It is not a matter of uncovering a crypto-Marxism or a socialist vein hidden beneath this delirium: Brisset upholds the *people* at a visceral level; and when we speak of class struggle, it must be understood as it was understood by the Romantic historians – Thierry, Michelet – or by writers of the people such as Vallès. For all of them, the *language* was a decisive stake, the locus of a symbolic confrontation between a people and privileged citizens. By dethroning Latin and Sanskrit, Brisset inscribes a hitherto separate political vision in his theory. As was the case for most of the philologists of his time, Brisset had formerly believed Sanskrit to be the purest of languages. But it was that very purity which came to render it suspect: too pure, Sanskrit could only be the language in which the discourse of the master was expressed.

It is not impossible that this change in perspective which displaced the entire economy and hierarchy of languages in Brisset's thought had something to do with the humiliation which Renan inflicted upon him by refusing to accept his linguistic work for the Academy competition. The challenge to Sanskrit would actually be aimed at the linguist. In order to press on in this direction, we would have to undertake an entirely different analysis, and note for example that the Romantics' love for the people, reinforced by the wound of a humiliation, seems to rejoin the classical paranoid theme of a love for the oppressed. This is all to be found in Brisset, as well as the clear traces of a sublimated homosexuality, a fear of persecution and a powerful narcissism – all of which are ingredients which contribute to forming the typical symptomatology of paranoia in the Freudian tradition, as set forth in the 1911 essay *The Mechanisms of Paranoia*.[40]

And it is certain that any attempt to understand the structure and the logic of Brisset's delirium, beyond its strictly logophilic dimension, must apply the principles of such a reading to the texts. We shall endeavour to do so in the following chapter, in order to explore more precisely the literal course of desire within a knowledge, at the heart of the enigma of the *sign*.

The key or the procedure

Enlightenment revealed a truth to logophiles: *the* truth; panglossia, as well as monoglossia, both symbolized and concretized the character of universality of each discovery: the entire language, all languages. The truth could thus be inscribed in an empirical field, and give rise to the establishment of positivities. All knowledge of the sign was in the service of desire, haunted by beliefs. But, in the process, vision and knowledge are riveted to one another. Mallarmé becomes a linguist in order to authenticate the way in which he lived the split in the sign; Saussure cannot dispense with his knowledge without risking the ever-present threat of an even greater madness; Roussel must mobilize all he knows about the language in order for his imaginary realm to bloom; Wolfson would literally be nothing if he were not profoundly polyglottic and a linguist; as for Brisset, we have just seen that the myth takes shape at the very heart of his science. If a 'delirium' is to be found in each of them, it is a *positive* delirium, rooted in a demanding practice which imposes precise and often highly complex methodological rules.

Yet, this very complexity is not exempt from a certain simplification. As we have reiterated, each logophile seeks a solution to a problem. The answer provided by the enlightenment is always a blinding shortcut, an organization which suddenly eliminates all the entropy from a complex system by enabling it to be conceived of from a single point. This point is at the same time a privileged *moment*, a unique *rule*, the victory of *a* subject who denies his split. Such a triumph of the unique is invested in the universal metaphor of the *key*. Owing to the key, something opens, a before and an after separate, a here and a beyond, a truth and an error, a knowledge and an ignorance: a *secret* is disclosed. All logophiles have known this phenomenon, which we have already seen take shape with extreme detail in Mallarmé's experience. We say 'phenomenon' for want of a better word, for it is an experience, something perhaps akin to 'chance' according to Bataille, an *event* which has a cognitive effect yet does not derive from knowledge, a structuring effect without being a structure, a productivity without object: something on the order of *différance*. The 'key' is what opens the instant to duration. And this corresponds quite logically to the structure of a knowledge which adopts a field whose unique rule presides over a system concealed beneath heterogeneous empiricisms. Meaning, structure, reality, subjectivity, all reside in the instantaneous. The successive, the progressive, the laborious are not located in that moment when everything is given at once in an immediate and total transparence, beyond time. Or rather, there is time, but it is the time of the gods, of the Verb, of that instantaneous creation after which everything else will drift or fall. Then knowledge as work will find its own time, its duration. Having become history, time will be able to unfurl in all its slowness transfigured by the memory of the experience of the original. This is the infinite testamentary development of a truth that can no longer be lost. The biblical myth of the fall and salvation, of the work of the good news, of the hidden course of divinity in man, *insists* in all these adventures. Brisset alone reinscribes its meaning in his own prophetism, but all rediscover the model.

In this perspective, the madness of the 'madman' is also that of the poet, of the scientist, of the mystic, of the philosopher; it is the pre-eminent human madness which Jacques Derrida so aptly described. It is a 'madness' internal to any knowledge which no exterior could contain; no science can completely repress it in the prescientific which would be its different and its other. No frontier resists it, and our notion of 'poetry' to which we seek to relegate it is not enough to protect other discourses from it. If all our sciences are semiotic, they will never be free from the madness of the sign. Saussure's case provides us with the most flagrant example. The irrationality of the anagrams would have given way to something like a pure science of the sign, with no remainder and no ties. Structural linguistics as a science would have suddenly been born, with its full epistemological dignity, upon the ruins of what had only been illusion, vagary. Isn't Saussure praised for having known how to refuse the seductions of a questioning of the origin, when founding his science? But what is the concept of *synchrony*, if not the translation into another discourse of the paradise lost, which was meaning immediately embraced by a secret in which the unity of the entire corpus of Latinity could be read? This may have been an effort to keep the question of the origin at a distance, but it became displaced in the investment of its inverse: the simultaneity which forms the unity of the network. It is not until Lévi-Strauss that a similar nostalgia will be betrayed in his supposition, furthermore inherited from Saussure, that language could only have appeared all at once and completely formed. The dream of the *Tristes Tropiques* is clearly a nostalgia for a before-Babel, a *Sehnsucht* which will have always tormented the Occident, before finally going mad in Romantic Europe, and being reborn scientific in anthropology beneath the gaze of that other who resembles us: the 'primitive'. The structure, or the 'key'.

The myth of the key – key to Paradise before the fall, kingdom of adventures and narratives – thus symbolizes the natural inverse of structural complexity, in so far as what the latter binds must become unbound and give itself, suddenly and without remainder. All doors open, the signifiers form the chain, a solidarity emerges, all words interpenetrate each other, a blossoming of fictions deploys at once all the figures of the imaginary suddenly realized. It is the end of the being separated. At the level of the structures, it means the end of intersystemic partitions. The 'key' is the hypostasis of Truth, but it is also the institution of a *law* – a fusion of epistemological and nomothetic values. Saussure provides a statement of this complex when he poses the profound identity of language and fiction, authenticated by the law. In this regard, he sums up the entire logophilic undertaking:[41]

> What accounts for the nobility of the legend as for that of
> the language, is that each, condemned to make use only of
> elements brought before them in any sense whatever, gathers
> them and constantly derives a new meaning from them. *A*
> *serious law presides*, which we would do well to consider
> before concluding that this conception of the legend is false:
> nowhere do we see anything bloom which is not the combina-
> tion of inert elements . . . .

The law presides over a formalism, and regulates the abstract or empty elements, always according to the same principles of a combinatory that transcends the empirical materialities. Or rather, beneath the practices operating in any language, the same calculation always emerges as responsible for the process of signification. Depending upon the field adopted by this calculation – one language, all languages – the meaning to be obtained can infinitely vary. This is the very law which allows for the English words as well as for the *Science of God, Locus*

Solus and the history of Wolfson; it is also that which permits the anagrams notebooks. Saussure uttered the law which orients his own procedure, as well as that of all the others: 'To imagine that a legend starts with a meaning, that it has had from its origin the meaning which it now has, or rather to imagine that it could not have had just any meaning, is an operation which exceeds my capacities.'[42]

But if every meaning is always a derivation, the aleatory product of some unspecified combinatory, how could Saussure have become immersed in the study of the Saturnian fiction, which is, after all, the perfect example of what the law permits to analyse? Saussure believed in the meaning which *preceded* the text, and failed to notice that, in imposing a retrospective meaning on that which could only be the product of chance and combination, he was succumbing to the belief which nevertheless 'exceeded' him. It does in fact exceed him, over-flow him, and, because of that, insinuates itself into the heart of his scientific reason: belief has perfectly invested knowledge. The *law*, henceforth misunderstood as such, returns in the form of the *key*: 'alliteration provided me with the key to the Saturnian . . . .'[43]

In the kingdom of desire, there is no place for metalanguage, no way of standing back to allow discourse to master discourse, no way of knowing what the practice of language does not know. Once desire has invested the form of the sign, it subjugates its entire field. From the beginning Saussure's desire had sought the sign and its combinatory, the senseless mark which thwarts meaning. The course in general linguistics would succeed in eluding the traps of the sign by reinventing a limit for containing it (the system, the structure), but this victory would have been won at the cost of an interminable labour around the law. This concern was already apparent in the years preceding the anagrams, as is manifest in this abstract by the Linguistic Society of Paris on 26 January 1889; we cite it in its entirety despite its length, as it is seldom recalled by paragrammatists:[44]

> Mr de Saussure presents a paper *on certain details of Homeric versification.* Excluding *cesura*, which he does not examine, he claims that a value is to be found at the *end of the word* 99 out of 100 times, which could not be attributed to chance; but, according to the claims of theorists of *cesura*, the latter could not explain the fact, since they constantly place it somewhere besides the third foot, and it becomes legitimate to operate, in a general manner, with the principle of the *end of the word*, whether this end of the word constitutes a *cesura*

or not, according to the wholly personal and precarious judgment of metricians. Having stated the principle, it is interesting to note that the first foot must as often as possible end with the end of a word (ὣς φάτο, etc.), which occurs approximately 55 out of 100 times; canto A is unique in this regard with 46 per cent and nearly comparable to the Batrachomyomachia, which reaches 44 per cent – Furthermore, we note the bizarre fact that the number of verses in which the first foot ends with a word is in an *inverse ratio* in each canto to those in which the fourth foot ends thus. When the first figure exceeds 52.5 per cent the other falls below 61.5 per cent, and reciprocally, without exception.

The expression 'inverse ratio' (*raison inverse*) is not used here without involuntary irony. With Homeric versification, Saussure experienced the rehearsal of the drama of the anagrams: 'a serious law presides', which distributes the combinatory without regard for the meaning of the words; an appeal is made to statistics – which is perhaps the reason for its absence from the anagrams notebooks, where it is evoked strictly as a possibility of authentification, albeit fruitless. And, finally, Saussure does not suspect the Homeric poet of composing according to occult rules, but the idea is present behind the entire analysis: all of this 'cannot be due to chance.'

Thus, what Saussure affirmed about legends, while thinking of the Niebelungen, is also what guides his reading of Homer, animates his research on the anagrams, and will finally serve as the theoretical foundation for the course in linguistics.

Such insistence cannot be 'due to chance', because it is the same law which upholds theories without apparent relation to each other, and which is even found to be at work in the science which disavows them. But Saussure's misrecognition does permit us to decipher beneath the key the very real *law* of the logophilic delirium, and not just the law of Saussure's 'delirium'. (But might we not ourselves be victims of this ambivalence: couldn't what we take to be a law actually be a *key*?)

It nevertheless remains true that whereas Saussure is content to establish a parallel, which he does not pursue, between the functioning of the *language* and that of the *legend*, he could have discovered that in reality, if there is a 'legend', it is precisely because the 'language' is as he describes it – 'a combination of inert elements'. Propp and the morphology of the folktale, structural anthropology applied to myth, all structural analysis of narrative derive from this conviction, the truth of which is proven by the very possibility of logophilia. What is

a logophile, if not a spirit animated by a certain belief, armed with a
certain knowledge about language, committed to the search for *meaning* at any cost (a meaning which does not pre-exist but which is given
to him *in addition* – but the logophile does not want to know this)?
For him it is then a matter of grasping a 'combinatory of inert elements', which he organizes and models into a legend, a myth, a fiction
in which he finally discovers the *proof* of his belief. Through such an
adventure, desire represents itself to him as a search for meaning, an
infinite quest within the signifier; when the belief has entirely developed
into knowledge, only the traces of the metamorphosis remain – but the
place is entirely theirs: narrative, poetry, theoretical novel. The very
structure of the language calls forth the legend, the myth, the *text*. And
the latter becomes a pure declension of its source, but a source which is
the very absence of any origin – or rather: the splitting of any origin, of
any presence. Desire thus throws itself into the spectacle of its own
différance. Saussure only inscribes his phantasy – and all the generality
of desire – in the play of a law which is the key to the 'key'.

Brisset's adventure, like that of Saussure, also consists of a sort of
theoretical epic whose end is the unveiling of the law. The paths
adopted by Brisset are not unlike those recognized by Saussure, but
the forms of exposition of his discovery are often much more complex.
In particular, when he revives the propositions of the eighteenth century, Brisset does not take the epistemological precautions with which
Saussure surrounds himself. What enlightenment directly reveals to him
goes beyond the recognition of a formal transcendence of the combinatory:[45]

> There exist in speech numerous laws unknown until today,
> the most important of which is that a sound or a sequence
> of identical, intelligible, and clear sounds can express dif-
> ferent things, through a modification of the manner of writing
> or of understanding these names or these words. *All ideas
> uttered with similar sounds have the same origin and all refer,
> in principle, to the same object.*

As the reduction of the empirical diversity of languages is a necessity
for Brisset, he must understand how the original unity and simplicity
of the Word drifted toward ambiguity. The only way to achieve this
consists of positing that language is in fact structured at two levels:
the 'surface structure', responsible for conventional, instrumental,
semanticism, and the 'deep structure', considerably simpler, which

gathers essential significations. But surface structure and deep structure must be understood here in terms of that which bases the articulation of the signifier upon a basic component: the phoneme (letter-sound). Thus, from the outset, the language is split, and every word obligatorily and constitutionally condenses two discourses; according to Brisset, to understand this, one must not dwell upon the troubling flicker of the apparent meaning, which deceives us. The true meaning of words is the sounds which compose them. 'Ideas' can form legitimate bonds only through the intermediary of their components in the signifier. Resemblances between ideas will be authenticated only if authorized by relations between 'sounds'. The signifier is the foundation for meaning. This discovery by Brisset (through which the entire problematic of the eighteenth century re-enters) is inscribed in the domain of a knowledge: it is a 'law of the Word'. But it is not only that: as we might have expected, it is also a *key*: 'This is the key which opens the books of the spoken word.'[46]

Linguistics and enlightenment are united in founding revelation upon science and truth. In this sense, Brisset becomes the perpetuator of hermeneutics, on the basis of identical beliefs. The most striking difference, however, is in the renunciation of the biblical privilege. The truth – doubtless a rare case in this tradition – can be spoken without a *text*, because the language is *already writing*, and even saintly writing. Further testimony of the radical logocentrism composing logophilia. Yet Brisset's logophilia differs in still another respect from hermeneutics in its institutional sense: the latter essentially adopts the domain of *discourse* as its own – an object in which Brisset contains only a superficial, and therefore derivative and profoundly inessential, meaning. As we have seen, if discourse holds a speech in its depth, it is surely beyond words that it can be heard. And yet what the words say are words – but words that are no longer those formed by discourse. What matters in them is the *idea*, and even more than the idea, the *object* revealed there: neither graphism nor signifying sonority, it is a *vision* that describes itself. What had consequently appeared at first to repeat the classical strategy of every hermeneutic in fact differentiates itself radically from it. Brisset's 'science' is in effect a crossing of signs which aims, beyond discourse, beyond the word, beyond the letter and even beyond the phoneme, for something on the order of the *spectacle*. The law serves only to dispose of the encumbrances of the sign, and becomes a *key* at the point when the treasure of prehistory has inverted itself: representation, instead of residing within language, is now where language comes to be inscribed – such is the work of enlightenment.

We are now at some distance from Saussure, but fairly close to Roussel. Even at the stage of the anagrams, Saussure does not in fact attribute meanings to sounds, to those phonemes which he isolates as the elements of a hidden poetic combinatory: these elements remain inert and acquire meaning only as an after-effect, in the constitutive movement of the text, of the structure – in short, of the myth. Thus, refusing to recognize a signifying function in the phoneme as such, Saussure is able to preserve the interlinguistic partitions characteristic of his monoglossia. The myth produced by his practice is but a precipitate of the latter; in itself, it remains wholly nonfigurative, and its direct products are always verbal products. The implicit identity of each language underpins this oblique prohibition. For his part, and under no circumstances, can Brisset recognize such an identity as a primary condition for the validity of an analysis. The logic of his theory of the language must transgress intersystemic frontiers in order to attain, without any acknowledged mediation, the transcendence of the spoken word, the pure presence of the origin. As a key, the law thus applies to something other than a status of the sign; it founds panglossia in its entirety: 'The Law stated above is a law of the spoken word and not a law of the French language; it applies to all languages and all dialects in particular. It applies to the whole of human language.'[47]

Saussure portrayed himself as the decoder of a derived truth, as the analyst of a process of composition – an admittedly phantasmatic one based upon an originally linguistic speculation, but one that retains its technical essence, except in the form of an historical investigation that would guarantee its truth, without being able to modify it. The situation is quite different for Brisset, who evolved from hermeneuticist to prophet. As he has deciphered what speech says, speech speaks through him; his narratives are the means whereby his vision becomes visible: he *is* the spoken word *and its theatre.* In a sense, he is not mistaken: the meaning which he discovers as the narrative of the origins, validated and guaranteed by the 'scientificity' of his methods, is the deeper meaning of the unspoken discourse which his unconscious desire had always held about its own origins. Projecting his phantasy about the supposed intentionality of the 'Word', Brisset's discourse will betray the combined effects of two, hitherto unpaired truths: that of Science and that of Desire: 'By analysing words we are thus going to hear the speech of the ancestors who live in us and through whom we live.'[48]

If there is something that Wolfson, literally, does not want to hear, it is that *voice*. The result he seeks is precisely the inverse of what Brisset strives to obtain he must, at all costs, prevent the slightest fragment of the English language (his mother's discourse) from penetrating his body, from invading that tenuous survival which constitutes his being. Every word heard in spite of himself would painfully remind him that this language also resides *in* him. His entire effort to remake a body of his own by rejecting English as an exteriority would crumble, the impossible foreclosure of the mother is incessantly annulled by the intrusion of a violent return:[49]

> But even when, having approached with the stealth of a wolf, she burst in like thunder and lightning, even at those times, the psychotic sometimes succeeded in plugging his ears before his mother had a chance to stick her head through the entrance in order, he thought, to look upon him as desperate, quickly trying to plug his ears while she continued to spout rapidly and at the top of her voice the words of the famous English language.

For Wolfson, panglossia, above all, takes the form of a certain investment of time, as the locus of the threat and of the defence. Panglossia permits a displacement, a means of fleeing to a safer position, in that it also requires the transformation of time into a network of instants. Wolfson is able to escape because he can always cross the instant in order to find safety on the other side of the language. Panglossia is a conquest of the instantaneous and of the outside; it is the very weapon of a subject combatting his phobia. In this sense, panglossia itself plays the role of a *key* for Wolfson, as a technique of signifying transmutation. It is the key with which Wolfson unlocks the freedom which awaits him outside – and he is obsessed with doors – just as Brisset's truth awaited him inside. Brisset's sudden unveiling is the respondent and the counterpart to Wolfson's immediacy, though the effects are inverted. Let us recall that for Saussure as well, the text was to be structured as an absolute simultaneity in the form of a network without gaps in which the seminal designation unifying the whole could be read. But the necessity for the constant availability of the entire network of languages at each instant is experienced by Wolfson in the mode of absolute urgency. His enlightenment – more so than in the discovery of his procedure – is encountered during each of its applications; it is a repetitive enlightenment which, weakening, would directly make him vulnerable:[50]

> as it was scarcely possible not to listen to his native tongue,
> he tried to develop means of almost instantaneously con-
> verting its words into foreign words each time that the
> former penetrated his consciousness in spite of his efforts
> not to perceive them.

Here, knowledge becomes science for Wolfson. This knowledge is already linguistic, since it was at the level of the other's words that he came to know his pain; side-stepping the words, seeking to defuse them, he acquires the ability to analyse them, hoping thereby to divest them of their capacity to make him suffer. The only path open to him is that of further developing his linguistic knowledge. But it is essential to note that this knowledge is neither disinterested, nor purely speculative; it is not a matter of attaining delight through rationality; on the con-trary, reason must be put to use in salvaging a *delight* which, alone, can authenticate him as a subject. Wolfson's belief is his desire to survive, and to this end alone he becomes a 'scholar'. The entire economy of his 'procedure' is knotted under the weight of this imperious fatality: he must have a system rich enough to foresee every eventuality and to hermetically suture any arrangement of phonemes susceptible to un-controllable occurrences that could give rise at any moment to *English*. What we have called enlightenment, the necessity for panglossia and the technical form of the procedure, impose themselves upon Wolfson as a single moment, beyond any dialectic. The procedure becomes a veri-table machine for converting signs, through the movement of an analysis which simultaneously translates signifiers and signifieds into something almost identical to what they were, but articulated in an entirely dif-ferent sign. The operation – which is more a process of conversion than one of translation – permits the identity of English to be melted in with the continuum – thereby instituted – of all other languages. Wolf-son's procedure can only rely upon a phonological decomposition, in the operation of which he rejoins all the other logophiles beyond the divergences which differentiated their strategies. But the metalanguage which alone permits us to grasp the nature of what has taken place there, is the one founded by Saussure when he stated his law on the combinatory of non-signifying elements. In this sense – and in this sense alone – Saussure is the pivot and the hinge for all of these experi-ences, the experience which permits all the others to be articulated for us at the level of a certain *technology*. He thereby rejoins Mallarmé, through whom the role of *desire* in all logophilia had become clarified. whom the role of *desire* in all logophilia had become clarified.

Throughout its progressive complexity, from the simple coupling of phonemes to the highly subtle construction of the *mannequin* or the *paramorph*, the elaboration of the system destined to filter the anagrammatic core in the texts where it hides can in effect only be conceived of in terms of a certain phonologism. Of course, it is all situated at a linguistic level (and in this regard Saussure did not invent anything), and especially at the level of the productivity of the system; the latter is possible only because a formal combinatory treats the products of the phonological analysis as non-signifying elements. Their reinscription in a network of rules alone permits the production of sequences bearing articulated significations. At the stage of the anagrams, Saussure had not yet quite reached this point: the particular meaning of the sequences thus produced was of less importance to him than their conformation, which made them recognizable or not. Recognizable, they prove the truth of the system; unassignable, they would prove that the latter had not succeeded in mastering entropy. The phonological analysis therefore has meaning only in conjunction with a system which permits the rearrangement of the phonemes collected in a text, like the elements in a rebus or a dream. This is an oneiric epistemology entirely subordinate to the re-production of the teleological figure which is (according to the theory) their veritable origin. In order to justify itself, the research had to impose such a limitation on its goals; if not, how could one decide among all the possible arrangements, each of which possesses an equal probability of occurrence, given the basic rules of the system? *Différance* has always worked upon this play internal to language, and can only propose for the combinatory a system of infinite referrals which only serve to manifest the creativity of the phonological principle that Saussure perceived as the emergence of disorder. The obvious requirement which consists of supposing words apparently belonging to the Latin language beneath Latin texts is not enough to make the system truly productive. This is why Saussure must append to the system a rule of restriction that excludes any combination which does not yield proper names. Given their low probability, these words are not entirely like other words. But religious, mythological, and literary overdetermination makes them privileged words; this is true to such an extent that, whereas highly improbable on the level of the pure linguistic combinatory, these words are eminently

85

probable if selected from a cultural lexicon. For example, Saussure will
not have to look far to find the highly probable name, Venus, beneath
the first poem by Lucretius.

In light of the theoretical consequences of his procedure (which he
attributes to the mysterious Latin poets), Saussure is, moreover, the
first to detect its ambiguities. But he does not seem to realize that,
beneath his procedure, the theory itself is what creates the problem.
Nevertheless, he will not take long to discover that he had erred in
selecting anagrams as his object; in order to avoid exhausting himself
in combating linguistic entropy with inappropriate means, he will pursue
the theory which could account for the reasons of his impasse: the
theory of the sign and of its 'arbitrariness'. He admits as much:[51]

> It is not only the *function of the anagram* (as such) which
> can be understood, without contradiction, in different ways;
> it is also its relation to the more general forms of the play
> upon phonemes; thus, the question allows for different solu-
> tions from every angle.

Pursuing his fascination with the syncope, with splits, with doubles,
Saussure almost became a *writer*; he did become one to a certain extent
if one admits that the anagrams represent an immense labour of re-
writing all Latin poetry. The concealed author whose figure he sought
to grasp was none other than himself. All literature became a mirror in
order for him to learn the meaning of his desire, the anguish of his
question. The withdrawal to science signals the end of the adventure,
but it took a sort of crime to permit it. In order to become himself,
Saussure, like Poe's William Wilson, had first to assassinate his double.
The Saturnian fiction is all that remains of his encounter with the
Uncanny inhabiting all langage.

Mallarmé, Saussure, Wolfson, Brisset, Roussel . . . . For each of them,
beneath the diversity of the textures, the phantasmatic impulses, the
strategies of desire, the same problematic is at work: a thought, sup-
ported by misrecognition, which bears upon the articulation of the
sign. A crossroads where linguistics, desire, and fiction interpenetrate
each other. At this level, every experience can be defined in terms of the
other, whatever the results; what we shall bear in mind are those traits
whereby the unique contour can no longer be surmised. As Saussure
states, there are 'different solutions' in this definition of the problematic cited above, which can serve as a model for the comprehension

of all whom we have studied. Among them, Roussel distinguishes himself in so far as he adopted 'imagination' as his field, and in so far as
what he produced can be inscribed with relative ease in a familiar
typology: we may be at a loss to classify the *Science of God*, but *Locus
Solus* is unequivocally a novel. Supposing that we really do know what
a novel is. None the less, his own *procedure* (this is what he calls his
technique) only appears to be a variation of the procedure postulated
by Saussure in his effort to become the author of all Latin poetry. As
a first step, he says: 'I selected two words that were nearly the same
(recalling the metagrams). For example *billard* and *pillard*. I then added
similar words but taken in two different ways, and I thus obtained two
nearly identical sentences.'[52]

Here we come upon Brisset or Wolfson's obsession with the resem-
blance which differs, or with the difference which assembles. For
Roussel, it takes a near-identity in order for something to happen,
which causes diversity to explode. He endlessly reinscribes the first
difference, the one which will apply to and justify all the others.
From this meticulously fashioned breach in the fabric of the language,
fiction will emerge, as when Brisset 'translated' the discourse of the
Word. But, whereas for Brisset the efflorescence of the spectacle
bloomed in the instant, its gestation for Roussel required perseverance.
Brisset learned to speak the language of the Word fluently, yet Roussel
never succeeded – and he perhaps never desired to, preoccupied as he
was with combining rather than producing new elements. Having produced words, he then had to produce 'stories' which combined these
products of a prior combination; and he would then need to apply
other, considerably more complicated rules. A producer of entropy,
Roussel is paradoxically more meticulous and more, in a word,
organized.

But, whether at the level of the narrative or at that of the elements
which serve as its primary matter, the phonological – or 'phonologistic'
– essence of his undertaking remains particularly clear. More sophis-
ticated than the approach of the first Saussure, it is also closer to the
differential vision of phonological phenomena characteristic of the
second. In summary, let us say that Roussel manifests the *double articulation of fiction*; it would still take linguists some time to discover
it in language.

The first stage of Roussel's procedure remains relatively simple,
since it entails his taking words that are in a sense one another's doubles,
while remaining separate; a single difference signs their similitude, but

difference and similitude are manifested by a concrete split. The second stage of the procedure goes much further in that Roussel will discover the invisible fissuration of *différance* at the very interior of each sign. All the terms he summons are in effect always already twin-faced, split, belaboured, deprived of identity because their *Other* inhabits them, strictly identical to themselves. Henceforth, each word can be Poe's William Wilson. If a difference remains, it is spectral, and not immediately textual, since it derives from the *signified* alone: [53]

> I selected a word and then linked it to another with the preposition *à* (to, for) and these two words, taken in a sense other than their primitive meaning, provided me with a new creation .... I took the word *palmier* (palm-tree) and decided to consider it both ways: in the sense of a *gâteau* (cake) and in the sense of an *arbre* (tree). Considering it in the sense of *gâteau*, I sought to wed it with the preposition *à* to another word, itself susceptible to being taken two different ways; I thus obtained (and this was, I repeat, a great and lengthy labour) a *palmier* (cake) *à restauration* (restaurant where cakes are served); which furthermore gave me a *palmier* (tree) *à restauration* (in the sense of restoring the dynasty to the throne). Whence the palm-tree in the Trophées square dedicated to the restoration of the Talou dynasty.

In this 'evolved procedure', as Roussel designates it, the words produce multi-dimensional networks in several directions at the same time. In passing to a matrix with four terms, the difference is considerably multiplied, and the fiction is freed of a constraint which obstructed it. In the first stage of the procedure, the fiction in effect developed between two fixed poles, and narrative diversification was possible only through internal differentiation, by means of embedding narrative sequences produced according to the same rule of production. Embeddings, plus the rule of recurrence, yield only a limited work of difference. Conversely, in the evolved process, a greater initial identity provides an infinitely richer outlet, since the rule of recurrence has been discarded: at the narrative level, the combinatory can be exploited in any direction. Which is true, of course, only if one does not take into account the regulatory codes appropriate to the genre chosen, and which will cause their own network of constraints to intervene. Initially respectful of constituted signs, despite some oblique infringements of the signified and the signifier, Roussel reaches the point of deconstituting them from within in order to inaugurate a general redistribution of their elements. It is surely in this regard that he becomes more authentically a writer, since the remainder of this operation, which became a sort of prosthesis for Roussel, a machine that could write in his stead, would be the discovery of the *supplement* which affects every sign and is set free by its fragmentation: narrativity. Or, according to Roussel's own usage, 'imagination'. In this final stage of his procedure, logophilia in its entirety can be recognized: [54]

> The procedure evolved and I was led to take a sentence at random, which I derived images from dislocating, a bit as though it were a matter of isolating the drawings in a rebus. Take, for example, the tale *The Poet and the Mooress.* There I used the song 'J'ai du bon tabac.' The first verse: 'J'ai du bon tabac dans ma tabatière' gave me: 'Jade tube onde aubade en mat . . . a basse tierce.' All the elements from the beginning of the tale can be recognized in the preceding sentence.

Language in its entirety has become fiction, and the working of writing envelops in a single movement the articulation of words and the liberated flow of the imagination.

4 Figuration of a delirium:
Brisset and the 'Science of God'*

Mallarmé initiated us to the detours of a history: an encounter between the sign and desire, writing and Nothingness. Mallarmé's entire delirium is bound in these folds, and it was there that we tried to understand what made up the destiny of *subjects* in logophilia. But it was Saussure who presented us with the key to such a delirium, in extracting from his own phantasy the formal core of a knowledge: the articulated structure of the sign, the 'arbitrariness' of its institution; he thereby showed us where the *science* of language was born. Science-*for*-a-subject: logophilia cannot be defined any differently.

There remains another aspect of logophilia, for which we tried to show the conditions of emergence, between desire and science, in the fracture of the sign; it is what we have designated by the global name, *fiction*. One should understand thereby a certain unexpected efflorescence, a certain sprouting that occurs seemingly at random and which saturates a field of vision with its plenitude: Hérodiade and the universe of the Dream for Mallarmé, the history of a freemasonry of poets for Saussure, the psychotic's novel for Wolfson, the marvellous adventures in Roussel's books, the history of man's ancestors for Brisset.

Of all these fictions, Brisset's is the richest, the most detailed, the most captivating – even more novelistic than Roussel's novels, because it does not seek to inscribe its productions in the field of instituted codes; more transgressive because, there, all desires are spoken, all reigns combined; more incisive because a passion for justice often transforms the narrative into a pamphlet with decidedly political resonances; more 'modern' because the mechanisms for the production of the text – its 'fictioning' – are the stakes which the narrative exposes as it unfurls. In attempting to reconstruct the logic of Brisset's delirium we may hope to clarify the link between the sign and fiction.

90

For a long time, the only things that were known about Brisset were his incongruous frogs, his ceremonial top hat, the trumpet of his seventh angel of the Apocalypse, his menagerie of gods and devils . . . .[1] The salient features of his linguistic system were also known: everything is in everything, the pun is the key to truth, the history of man can be plucked by anyone who so desires 'from the folds of the Word', in all the words of all languages.

This, from a distant reading intent upon a good laugh, is the final system, the comic opera of Brisset, his folklore. But systems – beyond the odds-and-ends of what they produce, beyond the pure forms of their calculations – also have a history and concrete structures to be understood, a certain form of causality that is both internal and external – as well as fissures, fractures, at times left out in plain sight, at others hastily jointed with new mythical expansions, elaborated for the needs of the cause. Mid-way between an abstract formalism and the incoherence of adventures at the surface, there is that strange place where transports and rigour coincide; something perhaps pertaining to discourse: zones of relative coherence that would very nearly correspond to the traditional classifications of knowledge. From this point of view, Brisset's work would therefore contain a general linguistics, an ontology, a political economy, a mytho-theology (a history), a zoology, a mysticism. We have tried to understand what sort of *procedure* made all this possible, but without raising a question about the nature of the phantasmatic which imposed its traits on the spectacles of the fiction, without asking ourselves how all of this held together. The following questions remain to be asked: What logic permitted this scaffolding to be erected? What opened up this work site? Where does all this lead? – in other words: what does it all come down to?

All the answers are no doubt there, in that discourse intent upon exhausting all speech, yet which never comes upon itself, lost in the labyrinth of its own involutions. Brisset never aims for the last word which would be the key to – or perhaps the end of – everything; he never turns back to face the disquieting evidence of what the spirit whispers to him. Thus, this entire discourse, the deluge of language would be no more than a vain noise destined to drown out that part of discourse which *must* remain unarticulated, even as it founds every articulation: an un-said, an un-thought, a chapter censored in the history of a man who brings the origins of man back to life in himself. That man: Brisset.

As a delirium, Brisset's paranoia is not confined to concealing the un-said; failing to say it, his delirium speaks of something else, which, nevertheless, persists in talking of the delirium. On this basis, we are able to formulate a series of hypotheses: Brisset's entire history (*his* history, but also the History that he reconstructs on the basis of it, his fiction) possesses at least two major poles, two catalysts of desire. The first is the *paranoia* as such, the set of specific conditions in which something happened to be repressed, and then returned, along un-published paths; politics in the broad sense is inscribed on the side of this pole: the body of Brisset's social resentments, perfectly discernible in the detail of his delirium. The same applies to a latent homosexuality, the numerous traces of which we shall detail. Speaking in this regard of paranoia we are adhering to a tradition, but we do so more to facilitate reading than to propose a diagnostic; psychoanalysis will be called upon here to fulfill its function as *myth*. The second pole will be that of *knowledges*: codes that are always already there, always functioning at the heart of deliria – established knowledges, established beliefs, which control them. This entire network, these borrowed systems, play for Brisset the role of ideological controllers, customs officials who authorize or refuse the crossing or the transit, like censorship at the threshold of consciousness, from which it is inseparable. There is a double unconscious: knowledges and desires, between which a subject traces his progress. On this side of the polarity being outlined, there will be a zoology, a biology – but also, of course, a theology and a linguistics.

These two poles ceaselessly strive to meet. Very early in the history of Brisset, their endless emissions of phantasies must have begun to crisscross and to interfere with one another; then, in the chaos of their confrontation, figures emerged, an order was gradually instituted, forming the base for new unpublished knowledge.

Reducing our hypotheses to their simplest form, we can posit a kind of purely indicative formula, which will summarize for us an entire psychogenesis, and with which we shall try to grasp briefly what was produced in the name of Brisset: paranoia + knowledges = mythology + science of God. We shall only be able at this time to outline the study of what pertains to the mythology as structure, and to paranoia as a history of the subject.

As noted in the previous chapter, Brisset is *enlightened* in the strongest sense. His texts are punctuated with ecstatic references to the Truth which suffused him, and he unambiguously poses this 'sudden and irresistible revelation' as the origin for all his subsequent science – for which he takes pride: 'It is a madness abandoned to enlightened spirits! You said it! It is an enlightened spirit who speaks to you.'[2]

Enlightenment was none the less not given to him once and for all, nor did it arrive uniformly. It is repeated, it returns in fits and starts, and each time amplifies and reveals new truths. But these truths are two-sided, for they conceal in proportion to what they reveal. For Brisset, all his research must strive to penetrate more deeply into the meaning of certain spectacles that have already been given. The first of all his enlightenments thus presents itself initially as a series of *scenes*, as the visual transcriptions of phonic chains, arranged in a ready-made formula, already given in the language as it exists prior to individual insertions. As with Roussel, we shall recognize here a certain transcendence of the stereotype, of the fixed syntagma:[3]

> Here is the *tra* formed. Here the shouts of the chiefs: *Tra in a*, tra forward. *Tra in ar*, tra backwards. *Tra deri*, to the right; *tra dera*, tra to the left; *traderidera*, to the right and to the left, pursue. *Tra, la, la*, here the fright; help! What immense emotion we felt when these scenes were presented to our spirit.

It is a theatricality of the signifier, which becomes song. The history of man begins with musical comedy, and this makes language an immense score. But what is this '*tra*'? It is a 'trait'. The translation does not stop there; panglossia gets involved to reveal that this 'trait' is also a *Drang*, a pressure. The same word is the object of another epiphany in the word 'ma traque' (*matraque* [club]), which designates in the language of the ancestors 'an immense willow bough'; 'in the hands of a robust man, it is a deadly weapon'.[4] What had begun with song quickly leads to other, more obscure zones: beneath the childish ritornello lurks a war chant, the promise of violence, the staging of power and of struggle. But this is not the only network which branches out from the simple word 'trac', for 'when the trait appeared, we knew that we were to be born'[5] – which is what we subsequently learn. A future birth is at play in the violence of combat. These scenes narrated in the present tense, the sudden emotion, the schema of evoked movements, the implied signifying links, shouldn't they all alert us to something beneath them to which they seem to be pointing: an entirely other scene seeking to describe itself through these words, a scene with its own meanings and its own links? The *primal scene*, perhaps? Something charged with emotion, on the order of a vision, is always found there. It is a fragmentary presence, distributed throughout the text, yet one whose inflexible rule will guide all of Brisset's research. In effect, everything will henceforth revolve around the word, but only to reveal that the sign is never arbitrary. Behind each sound that Brisset analyses, behind each signifier, a single signified emerges, one whose hypostasis is made increasingly transparent as the analyses progress: the *phallus*. At the very end of his research, in the final parts of his writings, Brisset will confirm the generalization which links the phallus and the sign to authenticate the subject; the universality of language, its truth and its only mooring, is the sexual member: 'The pronoun *I* designates the sexual member, and when I speak, it is a sexual organ, a virile member of the eternal-God which acts through his will or his permission.'[6]

The radical logocentrism of the logophile is compounded in Brisset by a no less crushing phallocentrism, for therein lies the thrust of all anthropology. Faced with the question: to be the phallus or to have it? , Brisset does not hesitate: both are true at the same time. His phallo-logocentrism thus describes the genesis of the signifier: 'Sexual sufferings are what drove the first ancestors to speak.'[7] 'Sexual force alone creates all human speech, as it does all humans. It also engendered all vices and all virtues.'[8]

We must make careful note of the fact that in Brisset's system, as we have stated, *there is no metaphor*; when he speaks of 'engendering', it must be taken literally. The consequences of this fact will be examined further on. In any event, Brisset could not be any clearer, and he thus presents us with one of the keys to his delirium: the discovery of sexuality is also that of language. Appearing together, forging their pathways in the same unconsciousness where they are together repressed and whence they together return, they reciprocally designate one another. More than with a return of the repressed, what we are dealing with here is a return of the *symbolic* as such, in the movement of a paradoxically *literal* metaphorization, a metonymy without difference. The phallus and the signifier are so close to one another that they may be, if necessary, mistaken for one another, in that gesture negating difference and the split, which we have identified as founding Brisset's analytical practice.

To explore words will be to know sex. The language race and logophilic curiosity make Brisset's theories an extension of 'theories of infantile sexuality'. This is also a struggle with phantasy, to avoid being circumscribed by its excesses: Brisset must detail it, fragment it, disseminate it, to tame it or to exhaust it in finding there all his *delight*. These are truths *à la Schreber*, set upon the other scene by the pathways of writing.

Let us leave behind, for the moment, this 'primal scene' which we interpret as the revelation of a coupling of the phallus and the signifier, of sex and the word – to the neglect of the biographical anecdote which may also seek expression therein. By itself, this original scene would not suffice to structure a delirium as rich as Brisset's. Other elements of analysis must be sought elsewhere; to this end, let us return to the enlightenment:

> 'One night in June in that same year of 1883, at the moment when, pensive, we were returning home, we felt an invisible man fall from the sky and penetrate us entirely.'[9]

> 'The more men penetrate one another, the more they become intimate in spirit, the higher they climb to the sky.'[10]

Knowing the literal functioning of what appears at first to be 'figurative' meaning in the discourse, we are in turn tempted to engage in that same practice which Brisset adopted to make words speak. But what we shall make them say will have little to do with the discourse unearthed by Brisset. The very lexicon of his delirium impels us to do so. Let us note, for example, that the word 'sky' is not indifferent to these texts: 'the first sky was the sexual member giving the water of the sky';[11] as for the word 'penetrate', it is easy to see that it is not introduced fortuitously; first of all, because of the literalness already stressed, but also because of the fact that Brisset repeatedly associates 'sky' and 'penetrate', as in the two examples given above. In the enlightened context of this entire adventure, instead of a 'penetration', we would have expected some hallucinated confrontation, a vision, a dialogue. No; as with Président Schreber, Brisset's enlightenment entails a possession from within. And it is carried out by a *man*.

This is the time to reread Freud, who wrote in reference to a case of paranoia manifested through symptoms linked to a delirium of persecution: 'The experience leads us to attribute to the phantasy of homosexual desire an intimate (and perhaps invariable) relation to this particular form of illness.' There seems to be little doubt here about the link. But we only avail ourselves of the Freudian schema to organize our reading; this schema also provides the following clue: 'The most striking traits of the origin of paranoia, especially in men, are humiliations and social vexations.'

Let us recall, in reference to the preceding observation, that Brisset had his share of bitterness, occasioned by a certain number of vexations, the most severe of which was surely that inflicted upon him by Renan, who refused his *Grammaire logique* at the Academy competition. Was this what provoked Brisset's definitive plunge into the paranoia which had only begun to take shape? Brisset's book did in fact come out in 1883, the year in which he claims to have first been enlightened. Failing to recognize what Brisset's effort was knotting between the science of the sign and desire, Renan would have condemned him to a dissatisfaction with the science of others, and to a need to construct his own in order to reaffirm himself.

There does in fact exist in all of his texts an omnipresent hatred for official scholars, the Faculty, the decorated, 'honourable men' – all of whom, for him, are agents of the devil and 'brigands'. The consequences of this hatred are profoundly political: it will call for the destruction of hierarchies and the proclamation of a future solidarity between all men. But the hatred for the decorated is not simply superimposed upon a delirium. Numerous anastomoses are traced between the two. For example: 'The rigid tail is the true mother of humans. Every honorable object is a visible symbol of this shameful animality.'[12]

There is nothing surprising in the fact that priests are the first to draw fire from Brisset's attacks; as with 'honourable men' in general, his hatred relies upon a signifying logic which provides him with the proof for his ideological prejudices; priests are scandalous because they always exhibit the *croix* (cross) (*'queue roi'*, *'queue roide'* [rigid tail]), and 'want others to kneel before them'[13] – for rites and reverences whose context allows it to be precisely understood that the sexual member, as is appropriate, plays a leading role: 'The adoration, which differs from the sacrifice, has its origin in a homage paid to the sexual member in a state of erection.'[14] When we come to the 'ancestors', we shall learn in fact that they took care of one another (*rendre les soins*) with 'their beaks'.[15]

Here, repressed homosexual desire does in fact seem to make its way into the detour of logophilic delirium. But it must be stressed that, in exploring this vein, Brisset never loses sight of the pivot of his construction, the equation signifier = phallus. On the contrary: '. . . all words were sucked, suckled, aspirated, licked and . . . there is not one that did not enter the mouth through one of these actions.'[16]

From there, Brisset goes on to construct an entire theory that will permit him to ensure the constancy of the truth of his equation. Throughout all activity of language, he will, for example, recognize a constant equivalence between *speaking* and *eating* (furthermore, a characteristic trait of other psychoses – among them, the case of Wolfson, whose relation to nourishment has been discussed). Eating will be the focus of a certain figuration of desire:[17]

> *Ange* [angel] is a call *au jeu* [to play], *en jeu* [in play], and to eating. *Meux en jeu* = put into the mouth. *Me ange* = my angel, *mange* [eat]. The angels performed for each other all the reciprocal services that were necessary to them. One did for the other, in the simplicity of his heart, what he would have others do unto him.

Here, Brisset seems close to *The Passionate Attraction* and to the complementarity of the passions as found in Fourier. But here we are only dealing with angels. The question of their sex is not even raised. Bisexuality? Asexuality? This question will come up later. For now, desire has given us its name; and when we know that, for Brisset, 'heart' = 'sexual organ', we can have a better understanding of the phantasy permeating these idyllic scenes so full of that purely evangelical innocence to which Brisset lays claim. These scenes furthermore provide an outlet for the coveted fraternal democracy which animates the political slope of his work; here we again come upon what Freud said concerning the 'erotic factor' which contributes to 'a love for humanity in general.' A homosexual bond at the base of the society of men, the solidarity of the sons in *Totem and Taboo*.

According to the revelations of the Word relayed by Brisset, humanity in its entirety was arrested at the oral stage; anthropogenesis can therefore be reduced to the positioning of a privileged anatomical organization, which serves as the support for the emergence of the symbolic – the indissoluble bond between *sex, speaking* and *'eating'*. The chain constituted by these three interchangeable terms is not presented in a theoretically articulated form in these texts, except in certain moments of extreme lucidity in the analysis. What surfaces most often in these 'narratives', in these readings of the Word, are fragments of the chain, certain ramifications at some remove from the junctures. In the *Logical Grammar* in particular, in which the structuring phantasy has not yet been fully exposed, we find a synecdoche of the oral stage in which the entire investment is concentrated in a typical displacement towards the *teeth*. One sentence adequately summarizes all the passages in which the same peculiar concern is evident: 'How little care man takes in general of his cleanliness, and especially of the upkeep of his teeth.'[18]

It is, moreover, significant that Brisset's first example of his procedure for analysing the Word – an apparently incongruous example – bears precisely upon a sentence in which the exercise of reading is presented as the declension of a paradigm in which the teeth predominate: 'We are going to read in this book, today open, what was hidden beneath these words: *the teeth*, the mouth.'[19]

Since the 'book' in question opens upon such words, we can well imagine that it is nothing other than the mouth itself. But the assimilation which establishes a profound similarity between the mouth and the book does not always proceed through analogy (the book is to words what the mouth is to speech); for Brisset, the point of contact which founds the analogy makes it a *literal* reality: '. . . the books are the lips (*lèvres*).'[20]

We wouldn't get very far if Brisset limited himself to simple transcriptions from one level of articulation to another: the system of the language on one side, the system of the body on the other, with communication between them facilitated by their *morphological* similitude. Not only are the body and the language isomorphous in the element of that kind of synchrony which constitutes their description, but they furthermore share the axes of the same history. Language is perfected as the body moves towards the fulfilment of its form. And what appears with language is the human universe itself, whose characteristic is the establishment of a moral typology. Brisset will therefore summarize all ontogenesis as a function of certain reference points which indistinctly blend physical realities, ethical realities and words. As when he computes the system of the emergence of teeth, seen as parallel to the establishment of sexuality and morality:[21]

> Until around the age of seven, children only have the dentition of the first ancestor and they also have his same unconscious awareness of good and evil. . . . From the ages of

seven to thirteen, as the second dentition develops, the spirit
is transformed into that of the devil, but with a knowledge
of good and evil. At the age of thirteen, the young man appears
and he is distinguished by a concern for the future. With his
wisdom teeth, the human animal is perfect.

Throughout this development, the intermediary of age permits a
form of numerology to establish the link between the formation of the
dentition and the formation of the body. Though transcendent, the
number nevertheless only functions for Brisset as a *word* – as is revealed
by the relation which he establishes between teeth and the sexual member: 'For a long time, the frog only had eight teeth in each jaw; the
arrival of the ninth (*neuvième*) tooth coincided with the perfect development of the sexual member: this was new (*neuf*) through and through.'[22]
In a general manner, all facts of morphology, whether they concern
the formation of the individual or the evolution of the species, will be
confirmed by corresponding facts in the language; this parallelism permits Brisset to translate what language says into what was the history
of the species. The latter in a sense recorded itself in the words which
accompanied it; all language becomes a *mystic writing pad* which functions according to the model of twin pathways as it was analysed by
Freud. A deep inscription retains the memory of the history of bodies,
a fragile inscription permits daily exchange. Brisset's 'Word' is the unconscious *in person.* Reconstituting in his analyses 'the formation of
the sexual organ', 'the arrival of the thumb', 'the development of the
neck and the arrival of hair', 'the arrival of teeth', or 'the formation of
the foot', Brisset does nothing other than explore the language as a
testamentary body, literally inscribed in the network of his phantasy.

As was to be expected, the sexual member would progressively occupy
a larger place in Brisset's fiction, and what had begun in the form of an
anatomical positioning would begin to take on moral resonances as the
'History' of man was further revealed. Thus, failing to differentiate
between the evolution of the individual and that of the species, this
historical development will take on all the characteristics of a veritable
drama: 'In acquiring his member, the frog little by little transformed
into a devil,'[23] a malevolent figure which devoured its children. Then,
'the demon thus became the ruler of the world, by virtue of its sexual
perfection.'[24]
Every word in the language is soon organized around this first phallic

point which distributes the relations between individuals on the basis of a strictly sexual violence of origin and of destination. In fact, the entire mechanism of powers comes to be irrigated by it, and Brisset's politics reconstructs every human society according to the principles of a libidinal economy which identifies the marking of bodies as the foundation of social constraints. Brisset exposes the archetype of this truth of politics in the guise of the 'serpentine ancestor' become 'hermit': [25]

> As soon as he held his overly trusting victim, he made her kiss the cross, slit her throat and then ate her. With the exception of the last act, we still find such monsters among the animals with human faces; the sufferings of others are their bitter delights.

In a general manner, and without always ending as it did in the description above, every social relation, every relation to the other necessarily passes through an oral operation: functions of chewing, of the beak, of the mouth. The diabolism of all these activities connected with orality is furthermore confirmed by this remark: 'Demons always have their hearts in their mouths.'[26] Sex, speech, 'eating'. Everything derives from them:

> The first thirty sounds of our language all refer, in principle, to the same object. Each says: take into the mouth, and designated the mouth where all the objects were placed, generally in the form of an eating;[27] to love was to eat;[28] They accosted each other by offering something in their mouths, and that is the origin of the kiss;[29] The sexual organ on fire is the first scourge . . . Yet, as soon as we are burned, an irrepressible impetuosity leads us to put the burn in the mouth and the fire is relieved.[30]

The link appears to be firmly established: Brisset's own sexual phantasmatic, with its patently homosexual component, blends in perfectly with the morphology characteristic of language. The words of the phantasy are the phantasy born of the words, as when Brisset writes that 'the madman (fou) who attacked a male from behind (derrière) gave rise to "mad with laughter" (fou de rire).'[31] Logophilia attains a limit beyond which it can only transform itself. Brisset will no longer be satisfied with these fixed 'views' revealed by the analysis of words, these scenes in the form of *tableaux vivants* which present themselves as historicized vignettes to be read like the frames of a comic strip; the next stage of the delirium represents a kind of visual take-off, the conquest of a kind of dynamic of enlightenment, in which the 'view' gives way to the *narrative*. From this moment on, the figures will be linked to produce the continuity of a plot whose logic develops in several directions: on the one hand, a production of the protagonists; on the other, a production of the evolution which derives them from one another. It is at this moment that Brisset's delirium is definitively transformed into a mythology.

The production of the *protagonists* condenses the entire phantasmatic; in particular the one revolving around the figuration of homosexual desire. Among the principal characters are the distinct figures of the *devil* and the *demon*: 'The angels and archangels were the good demons and the good devils, just as the demons and devils were the bad angels and archangels.'[32]

But, the essential trait in the character of the demon was his sexual member: 'The *demon* showed his dice, his dais, his deity, his sexual member. He grew proud of his nudity. He required abject services, and did not care to submit to them.'[33]

Here we find other themes evoked in other contexts presented with considerable concision: 'Almost all human speech presents this origin, and this is one of the first points to manifest itself in our deeper thoughts. The shout *que* [that] or *queux* [tail], especially, depicts a being who calls to his ass.'[34] Besides, 'the first postal service was on the friend's back.'[35]

The same *a tergo* staging accompanies the formation of the being that was to become the principal protagonist of the entire history of man; the *frog* – a complex figuration of sexual differences, in so far as it is both wife and mother, and entirely subordinate to the phallic law:[36]

> The *raine* designates the frog and it is by this name that I
> first knew her; the arena (*l'arène*) is the name for sand (*sable*)
> where, above, we saw the devil (*diable*). The devil on the
> arena (*sur l'arène*) was also on the (*sur la*) *raine* and this
> *raine* that was the first mother, became the woman raised
> to the highest level of dignity, she became the queen (*la reine*).
> In the plural, we can see that they held the *raines* from be-
> hind by the reins (*rènes*) which were their own arms. Once
> they were held by the arms, the devil dominating them led

them about at will. Queens are therefore by their nature subordinate to the devil.

With devils and queens, which pose at their own level the mystery
of the masculine and the feminine, the question of birth, and the problem of power and violence, Brisset is equipped to undertake the
reconstruction of the entire history of man throughout the network
of speech. It is not surprising that this investigation of history coincides for Brisset with an investigation of his own history, where two
fundamental discoveries emerge at almost the same time: the discovery
of the *frog*, on the one hand, and the discovery of the *tongue*, on the
other. Two passages permit this original and seminal coincidence to be
established: [37]

> Around the age of eleven, we came upon a frog and, with
> the cruelty of a scamp, crushed it with a wooden bough [Let
> me recall 'ma traque' which was made of an 'enormous willow
> bough'] pressed against its belly, when the poor beast, suddenly
> spreading its arms and legs, struck us with amazement. We
> dropped down to get a better look: it looks like a person, our
> spirit suggested, and we went away astonished, pensive, and
> repenting of our barbarity. For it goes without saying that the
> frog already has all the corporeal characteristics of a charming
> little human being.

The 'already' is the source of the entire idea of a diachrony crossing
the species and joining the bathrachian to man in a continuous evolution. Here, in the biography, we come close to that moment when
Brisset first put together everything that he would later shape into a
mythology. The second shutter of the phantasy is the necessary logophilic discovery which is also 'already' present in Brisset's preoccupation
– although still without effect: [38]

> I was twelve years old. Today, almost at the door of old age,
> the man can speak of the child as of a stranger. The soul of
> the child was avid for a knowledge of languages. In the midst
> of the fields, having read all he could find, his spirit sought
> nourishment on all sides. A jargon utilized in the village and
> almost lost despite two or three initiates, had enabled him to
> construct two others. But this did not satisfy him, this was
> not a language. Then, in order to have entirely unrecognizable
> words, he changed the place of letters, putting the last at

the beginning: *bread* was *dreab; house, eoush*. It was incoherent
and had no object whatsoever . . . .

This was a logophilic apotheosis in which Brisset encounters Saussure, Roussel, Mallarmé, Wolfson, and through which his delirium takes
shape at the intersection of an anxiety and a knowledge.

The frog is therefore the dream object – in every sense of the term –
the perfect condensation of everything which pertains to the formation
and the transformation of the phantasy. Therefore on the basis of and
around it, Brisset builds his entire mythology; it is the enigmatic
figure of sexual differences and the origin of speech. The history of
the frog will be a sort of family romance for Brisset, a reinterpretation
of his own history and a justification for his mis-recognized desires.
The entire logic of the language becomes the logic of his phantasies.

As in every mythological figuration, there exists in that of Brisset
an extremely complex system which attempts to restore in a regulated
manner an entire genealogy of the species, intimately blended with a
genealogy of the gods. Some attempt must be made to reconstitute,
to describe and explicate the 'elementary structures' of this kindred
phantasmatic. Let us begin with the summary which Brisset himself
provides:[39]

> We have seen creation develop from the Germination of
> the frog; we have seen this small animal already capable of
> speech, grow, acquire sexual organs, disengage its head from
> its shoulders, and thus be groomed and crowned. The thumb
> emerged to complete the fingers and we counted two dozen
> teeth. Finally, this ancestor, perfected in the devil, united with
> a raine or frog equally equipped with sexual organs, and from
> their embraces were born the first gods and goddesses. These
> gods, children of the devil, and these goddesses, daughters of
> the raines-mothers, in turn united and the unwed-mothers
> (*filles-mères*) gave birth to gods and goddesses who be-
> come kings and men when they stood up on their feet.

Let us see how these transformations – Brisset is a transformationist:
he refuses Darwin's evolutionism – articulate the stages. Let us note
first that, surprisingly enough, man has not *one* but *two* mothers: 'The
raine-mother is the first mother of man, the grandmother. . . . The
second mother of man is the unwed-mother.'[40]

We must therefore take into account the fact that man possesses a simultaneous double origin, a dual system of filiation – which corresponds to the distinction noted above between two periods in the life of man, that of the ignorance of good and evil and that of the formation of the ethical personality. Beyond that, there is the problem of the difference between the sexes, between the two levels of the language, the sign, and finally the very one which again splits man. All of which is symbolized in the double nature of man: 'In so far as he is a god, man is the son of the raine-mother and the devil; in so far as he is a man, God is his father, and his mother is an unwed-mother.'[41]

The solution to any aporia requires that one go beyond it to derive unity from division, and similitude from dissimilarity. This is the logic of compossibility, which can only reside in language, with the complicity of signs which guarantee with their materiality the truth of the objects invented by desire. This is how, in Brisset's vision, man can be *both* man and god. There is none the less a qualification: 'The god is child-like, it is not a perfect being. There are no perfect animals besides the devil and man.' But then, whence the difference? In this instance, Brisset's explanation is not entirely based upon the logic of the language, since the barrier between the child and the man, the god and the devil, is the sexual member. But we know that this member is nothing other than the word, nothing other than the subject. Despite appearances to the contrary, the establishment of human genealogy therefore denies nothing of the heuristic procedure hitherto practised. *All* histories are joined in that procedure: that of speech and that of man, that of Brisset and that of God; the form of their encounter predictably finds the Oedipal scenario:[42]

> Every king is a rebellious son to God who wants no other king than man, his only son. Every king who is the son of a queen-mother (*reine-mère*) is the son of a raine-mother (*raine-mère*), and consequently a son of the devil. The son of God cannot be subjugated by a child of the devil.

The history of man divulges a sombre family plot, in which the principal criterion clearly appears to be the question of legitimacy and power: 'If the devil admired the raine-mother, he was horrified by the unwed-mother, for it was the latter who signified that he was henceforth relegated to an inferior rank.'[43]

It is difficult here to fail to recognize the urgency of a desire playing out the drama of its origins through words. The analysis of the language may have produced the actors and the logic of their interrelations, but the pathos of their loves and hatreds could only have come from the investment of a subject preoccupied with remaking his own history. Is it Brisset's family romance that has always been inscribed in the language? We can sense the return of a concealed biography, nevertheless present in the fiction which effaces it: 'The gods never married; they never formed bonds; but generally a god would adopt the child of an unwed-mother and become attached with his entire soul to this child, and by that fact become its true father.'[44]

Brisset or the natural son? This could explain a mythology which doesn't know what to do with one father *too many*. Man therefore appeared in two phases. During the first phase, he was produced by sexual reproduction but he had no member; he had been castrated by this phallus-father that he could not be. During the second phase, he rebels, refuses the impasses of such a birth and is reborn as the child of an unwed-mother; he is henceforth man and god, after having acquired both his sexuality and a true father who rids him of the other, child of the devil and the devil in person:

> The first god, like the first animal man, had no determined male as a father. He only knew with certainty the mother who had suckled him.[45]

> The name of the father is given only to God the Father. Every other father is a devil; he stalks about everywhere seeking to be called the father, my father. Yes, he dares take the name of the father before the heavens, he seeks God's place on earth.[46]

We can see it clearly: the entire genealogical revision elaborated by Brisset has one essential goal: to make the (one) father disappear, 'to destroy the infernal monster who was our first father and who lives in us, the sanguinary beast'.[45] Beyond logocentrism and phallocentrism, familialism is what intervenes in logophilia, to even the score with the Name-of-the-Father, in the very midst of the symbolic. Castration and seduction spring from the sign, and logophilia as a whole is an Oedipal complex:[47]

Reader, who art a man, reader, who art a woman; if your

mother, in her turpitude and deviation, were to show you,
in the absence of your father, another gentleman, the devil,
her lover and were she to ask you to love him, serve him, and
obey him as your father, would you do it? If you were to do
so, with what eye would your father view you upon his
return to find his place taken in the bed of your mother and
in your heart? Would he not seek out his faithful son or sons
to drive the foreign beast from the house, along with the
mother and the unworthy children?

There clearly is this Oedipal structure, but it is a paradoxical one,
since he can *both* drive the father away and restore his rights. Is this
a miracle of the Word or the nudity of the biography? It is doubtless
one and the other, for it will have taken the complicity of words to
appease the conflict in a fiction.

As we have noted, the frog had already been set up as a crossroads in
the elaboration of the myth. There were numerous reasons for this,
and we have only evoked some of them. There is one, however, which
seems to be especially important, in the light of its logophilic implications.

Evidencing his panglossia, Brisset knew a great number of languages,
but he also knew argot extremely well. There is evidence for it on each
page. He consequently could not have been unaware of what the word
'grenouille' (frog) also meant in nineteenth-century Parisian argot. A
dictionary of that period defines it as 'the generic name given to the
small loose population'. In other words, a 'frog' was also a lower-class
prostitute. This meaning is reinforced by the link between this word
and another, which Brisset himself points out: *'gouine* [dike] is a syno-
nym for frog, in the figurative sense.'[48] Yet, for Brisset, the 'figurative'
is always to some extent literal. This does seem to complete the Oedipal
tableau, but it entails a notable displacement which makes Brisset's
phantasmatic a conjunction of two 'complexes': the figure of Oedipus
blends with that of Electra. We can well imagine the labyrinths his
desire had to travel to maintain its own existence between two fathers
and a mother who is both adored and accursed. Perhaps we will discover some day, when there will be a *Life of Brisset*, that the specific
solution which he invented was woven from the encounter of these
impossibilities, by causing the mysteries of the language to coincide
with those of genealogy, beyond a generation: 'The raine-mother is
the first mother of man, the *grand-mère* [grand-mother]. She was

the first to teach the child to speak and was the first *grammaire* [grammar].'[49]

The mysteries of sex are thus spread throughout language, and all it takes is to investigate its grammar. But what is Brisset's own sex? The question is an impossible one which would require unravelling all the threads of the delirium. He perhaps wants to be both 'frog' and 'devil' – both man and woman; but this would carry desire back to that epoch before knowledge in which the two sexes were unified in the absence of sex. This would consist of a foreclosure of the phallus which, as is to be expected, returns in the very course of the real, having become every sound, every word, every object, the entire body, the complete man. This is a time of profound tranquillity, but one that is soon disrupted by the eruption of that diabolical member:[50]

> The thing which one recalls (*rappelle*) the most deeply, if one has not been prematurely debauched by circumcision or otherwise, is the peeling of the rat (*pelage du rat*), the baring of the prepuce. As the ancestor was surprised by violent erections, his rat peeled (*rat pelait*), *crowned* itself bit by bit, *pope*, and he experienced pains analogous to those of the virgin torn by the peeling rat (*rat pelant*).

We saw earlier that the remedy for all these pains brought on by the 'member on fire', was fellatio. But, prior to the determination of an object-choice, these pains were especially the support for an identification which does seem to put the image of the mother into play. As for her, she, of course, could only be *virgin* and *mother*, both of which functions have been determined by the phallus itself, the '*rat pelant*': 'Virgin (*vierge*) or penis (*verge*), it is the same word. The word *vierge* passed from the *verge* to the first ones who knew love and became mothers.'[51]

Besides, 'the ancient French law, written in Latin, in speaking of questionable paternity, clearly says: *Virgini parturienti creditur*: you must believe in the virgin in labour. This word thus had the value of unwed-mother.'[52]

We have come full circle and we again find the phantasy which governs genealogy with the help of the language, which proves its validity. Brisset has proven that which he kept trying to find a way of demonstrating at each step of his analyses: one can *be* the phallus, deny oneself as such, *have* it, and be possessed by it in so far as one does not have it. In Brisset's case, paranoia would thus be accompanied by a fundamental bisexuality, which expresses a latent homosexuality as well as a desire for the abolition of sexes. This was true as well of the frog: reproducing asexually, it could, in the phantasy, be neither one sex nor the other, or else both at the same time. Whence the different epochs of man, and his very particular relation to *delight*:[53]

> the male and the female had the name d'*on*, d'*homme*. The big lump of a woman (*grosse dondon*) was an *on* in the wave (*onde*). From the wave (*D'onde*) *on*. The name *man* (*homme*) has the same origin, and it designated two equally sexless beings. The spiritual man has no sex(ual organ).

Throughout his entire research, Brisset strives to assure the return and apotheosis of this man: '. . . the most perfect sky is the soul of man and woman profoundly united and forming but one being.'[54]

The Science of God speaks to us of this paradise regained, the place 'where men and the beasts spoke together'. This is the kingdom of fiction, the place without a locus, whose only theatre is the *word*. Exposing this utopia, Brisset establishes himself as the most striking of the logophilic adventurers: the figuration of a delirium whose sole resource is the fecund poverty of the sign.

Conclusion

Neighbouring concepts, nearly identical procedures thus serve the different logophiles in a variety of different ways, profoundly different in their results and in the texts they permit, yet profoundly kindred in that each raises the same question of desire and the sign, sex and the word, of the subject and of the language. From having lived the adventure of this impatience and this anxiety, Mallarmé finally derived something like a poet's 'work', which was endlessly at the limit of its own absence. Face to face with the sign which makes poetics and writing the stakes for well-being and knowledge, Mallarmé thus locates for us the historical *and* personal enigma of *literature*. Mallarmé writes, and therein lies his entire research: the mystery of an intransitive language.

Saussure does not write; he rewrites. Taking a given text, he locates phonological regularities and seeks to clarify the reason behind them, but against the grain of reason. He wants to verify their authenticity and their reality beyond a flickering which ensnares him like a misunderstood lure. In order to do so, he must suppose an initial sequence of phonemes, and establish a hierarchy of transformations, of transformational rules capable of producing an adequate description of the effective structure of the terminal text. This was the operation of a formal give-and-take, of encoding and decoding, but especially of self-verification. It was also an interminable operation – in the Freudian sense of an 'interminable' analysis, and precisely for the same reasons.

As Saussure discovers, all words, in the limitless network of the forms of the language, can have, or be, the last word. This is a process in which language is pulverized, in which the subject and his reason are lost, in which history is remade. In turn, the terminal text starts working, germinating, since it is but the new nodal formula of a text through which Saussure unwittingly applies himself to a task of writing which becomes a veritable theoretical fiction in which the contamination inscribed in every language is exposed: constitutive corrosion of its paradoxical nature. Writing takes hold of what seeks to hold it, and sweeps it away in an endless vertigo.

Wolfson, as well, becomes the impassioned and absent memorialist of his own procedure, the shaky hero of a narrative which is the history of a system of kinship assigned to all languages on the model of a true kinship whose symbolic consequences he, as subject, refuses to assume. Brisset likewise ends up writing a text which is both his theory and the fiction which it produced, the myth it allowed; but it is the desire concealed in the fiction which returns to uphold the theory's necessary choices. And Roussel in turn goes through those same stages, then leaps directly into the fiction which they permit to blossom, and which he prefers to keep hidden until the moment when a new narrative imposes their revelation: moment of the testamentary *I*, which seals his adherence to the text which wove his life.

For each of the logophiles, having recognized and gone beyond the simple level of signs, articulated and modulated by the network which moves signifiers and signifieds, it is as if language alone could not detain meaning and the subject upon this quotidian and coded surface. On the one hand, meaning overflows toward the microstructure and, having disarticulated signs, takes hold of the phonemes; on the other hand, yet at the same time and in the same gesture, the logophile reappropriates these dislocated elements and rearranges them in new chains that will run beneath the surface of the neutralized ordinary language to consolidate unpublished meanings, new intrigues, configurations whose only debt will be to the rigorous caprice of desire. The theatre is an internal one: the intimate scene of the sign. There, enigmas are formed and discovered, and desire, having submitted the whole of the language – all languages, language in its entirety – to the promptings of primary process, suddenly invents a new dimension which will constitute the text as a veritable *tertiary* process. In a single disoriented space, consciousness and unconsciousness, language and history are played out and bound together – just as, at the level of the analysis of the language, the second articulation gives way to a third in which the first two are blended; from the phoneme to the mytheme through the fracture of the sign.

Such extensive corrosion finally coerces language and all languages to divulge their secret: the 'arbitrariness' of the sign, the nothingness articulating it, the combinatory infinity at the heart of this nothingness crawling with narratives. The language is a chaos of atoms in which the *clinamen*-desire brings forth the figures of the World, the meaning of a universe for a Subject. This reveals the infinity of meaning, which desire will henceforth pursue, like an enticement which it has created for itself, throughout an interminable text which it invents in order to effect the reunion with itself which it will forever be denied. For the final meaning is never stated, the last pathway never found: there are no more impasses, no more holes, nothing but a surface, a ramification of series whose proliferation can no longer be arrested. The nothingness of the sign, once discovered and turned over, takes on the aspects of a vertigo – the menacing plenitude of *madness*. But there the paths suddenly diverged. Mallarmé avoided the threat by withdrawing to the science of language. Saussure followed this same path, and perceived madness from afar, once he had become settled in a knowledge which allowed him to translate the vertigo into a reassuring certainty. But he had first to encounter uncertainty:[1]

> When a paragram appears, it seems a ray of light. Then, when we see that we can add a second and a third, rather than experience relief from our doubts, we begin to lose that absolute confidence we had had in the first: because then we begin to wonder whether we could not definitively find all possible words in each text . . .

Clearly, this is where the truth of the embrace between language and desire is stated. Yet, unlike Saussure, Roussel delights in what this same discovery signifies for him: unrestricted access to an automatic and inexhaustible source of literature. Roussel thus adopts the point of view of the producer of fiction – in fact, of *all* producers, since it is he who makes them possible by generously unveiling to all what the veil of Isis had concealed. A *writer*: that is what he had wanted to be ever since the moment of his 'enlightenment', whereas Saussure, cloistered in his role of linguist and academician, never imagined for a moment that the procedures he had discovered could be generalized and put to creative use. Dead language and dead literature are the only field made available to him by his imaginary order. For him, the opening of the sign gapes upon the forever-sealed closure of a lost practice that would necessarily be exhausted once it had been fully explored. Where Saussure sees only a progressive saturation, a gradual engulfing of the play

111

of the signs, Roussel points the way to a perpetual unfolding: 'this procedure, it seems that it is my duty to reveal it, for I have the impression
that all writers of the future could perhaps fruitfully exploit it.'[2]

Is it the specificity of their ideological and social 'casting' that, in
the case of each, prescribes or forbids certain intuitions, certain visions
or certain volitions? The fact remains that, even in unreason, Saussure
is still a philologist, Roussel a writer, Mallarmé a poet, and Wolfson a
psychotic. Confined from the outset in his 'occupation' as 'squizo-
frenic' and in spite of his career as a 'student of languages', Wolfson
will never get out; psychiatrists will condemn him to invent nothing
with his method but stories of madmen and family romances.

Brisset alone seems to have escaped his original limitations to a
certain extent: within his delirium there remains little trace of his past
as a police officer, and almost nothing of his grammatical exercises. The
only thing left is this marvellous, delirious machine which tells us the
Arabian nights of the ancestors of man, the intrigues, the wars, the
loves and feasts of the gods and the devils, the adventures of the frog.
But this is because Brisset sacrificed everything for his dream of a total
epiphany, for the visions of his definitively deranged desire. He represents what he writes for himself so that he may identify with it, become
the Truth which the Word proclaims through him, and which he alone
was able to unveil, achieving thereby his apotheosis as an Archangel of
the Apocalypse:[3]

> The work which we conclude with these lines is the opening
> and the part of the book of life of chapter twenty of the Apo-
> calypse, verses twelve and fifteen. It contains the first leaves
> of the tree of life of the garden of Eden which Moses wrote
> of three thousand five hundred years ago, and of which John
> also spoke in the final chapter of his sublime revelation more
> than eighteen hundred years ago. It is the key to the book
> sealed by seven seals which none was worthy to open, save
> the lamb who was immolated; no one could even look upon
> this book; that is, have an idea of its formidable existence.

The innocent victim which had to be immolated for the 'infinite'
to be discovered in the flow of its blood, is it not that which, in the
adventure of the logophile – of which Brisset, Mallarmé, Saussure,
Roussel, and Wolfson are but the ephemeral figures – best designates
the innocence of the sign, which must in turn be fractured to discover
the infinity of the text in the rout of its meaning?

Depending upon the slope of one's desire and the nuance of nothingness to be discovered there, to touch upon the sign may be to go towards madness, science or literature: triple destiny of the psychotic, of the linguist or of the poet, bound up in the same enigma.[4]

Notes

The fiction of the sign

1 A term coined by Lacan and recently used in his seminar. See recent issues of *Ornicar* (published by the Department of Psychoanalysis of Vincennes University) for transcripts. Also J. - Cl. Milner, *L'Amour de la Langue*, Seuil, 1978.

2 Cf. in particular the study by Luce Irigaray: *Le langage des déments*, Mouton, 1968, as well as 'Expression et Signe' by the same author, in *Études psychologiques*, vol. 1, 1971.

3 Cf. C. Delacampagne, *Figures de l'oppression*, P.U.F., 1977.

4 In *Poétique*, n. 11, vol. 3. Todorov proposes a classification into which would be inscribed the linguistic theories of those to be studied here from the standpoint of the logic of their delirium: etiology of their semiology. In addition to this effort at linguistic classification set forth by Todorov in the article entitled 'Le sens des sons', we shall find a useful complement to any study of logophilia in J. C. Lebensztejn's book, *La Fourche*, Gallimard, 1972, in the form of an exhaustive exploration of the combinatory permitting anagrammatic permutations. C. Delacampagne *op. cit.* also confronts some of the problems studied here. Jean Roudaut's book, *Poètes et grammairiens au XVIIIe siècle*, constitutes an indispensable reference for any discussion of paragrammatism from Court de Gébelin to OU.LI.PO. The series of studies published by G. Genette in *Mimologiques*, Seuil, 1976, is an important source of information, even though Genette did limit his study to a strictly linguistic analysis of the theories of De Brosses, Court de Gébelin and Nodier. Julia Kristeva's work on Roussel, Mallarmé and paragrammatism in general, published in *Semiotiké*, Seuil, 1969, and *La Révolution du langage poétique*, Seuil, 1973, should also be mentioned for the link which they established between logophilia and modernity.

5 In his essay on Maurice Blanchot, published in *Cahiers du chemin*, 1974.

6 *The Prison-House of Language*, Princeton University Press, 1972.

7 Painting by Moritz von Schwind, commented upon by Freud in his *Introduction à la psychanalyse*, and reproduced on the cover of the special issue of *l'Arc* (no. 34) devoted to Freud.

8 Mallarmé, *Oeuvres Complètes*, Pléiade, 1945, p. 69.
9 Cf. J. Lacan, 'Encore', *Seminaire*, Seuil, 1975.
10 Kristeva, *op. cit.*
11 Cf. the trend of semiotic studies exemplified by certain articles published in the past few years in *Semiotica, BLS*, etc.
12 During an interview conducted by the *Quinzaine littéraire*, on the occasion of the publication of a new edition of Auguste Comte's *Cours de philosophie positive*, Anthropos, 1975.
13 Mallarmé, *Correspondance*, vol. I, 1862-71, 6th edn, Gallimard, 1959, p. 220.
14 Cf. Roudaut, *op. cit.*
15 Mallarmé, *Correspondance*, p. 240.
16 *Ibid.*, 31 December 1869, p. 315.
17 *Ibid.*, 31 March 1871, p. 342.

1 Mallarmé's madness

* There will be no references found here to such well-known studies of Mallarmé as those of M. Blanchot, J. Scherer, J. - P. Richard, R. Cohn, M. Foucault, J. Derrida. They would have been too numerous; which should convey how much this essay owes to them.

1 Dr Jean Fretet, *L'Aliénation poétique*, J. - B. Janin, Paris, 1946.
2 Mallarmé, *Correspondance*, 6th edn., Gallimard, vol. 1, 1959, 28 July 1866, p. 225.

3 *Ibid.*   4 *Ibid.*, 16 July 1866, p. 222.
5 *Ibid.*, 24 March 1871, p. 347.   6 *Ibid.*, 4 June 1862.
7 *Ibid.*, January 1864.   8 *Ibid.*, July 1864.
9 *Ibid.*, November 1864.   10 *Ibid.*, 31 December 1865.
11 *Ibid.*, 20 March 1865.   12 *Ibid.*, 23 August 1866.
13 *Ibid.*, 17 May 1867   14 *Ibid.*, 8 August 1867.
15 *Ibid.*, 7 October 1867.   16 *Ibid.*, 20 April 1868.
17 *Ibid.*, 3 May 1868.   18 *Ibid.*, 4 December 1868.
19 *Ibid.*, 31 December 1869.   20 *Ibid.*, 3 April 1870.
21 *Ibid.*, 3 March 1871   22 *Ibid.* 6 November 1864.
23 *Ibid.*   24 *Ibid.*, January 1865.
25 *Ibid.*, 14 May 1867.   26 *Ibid.*
27 *Ibid.*, 24 September 1867.   28 *Ibid.*, 17 May 1867.
29 *Ibid.*, 22 May 1870.   30 *Ibid.*, November 1864.
31 *Ibid.*, May 1865.   32 *Ibid.*, 8 August 1867.
33 *Ibid.*, 24 September 1867.   34 *Ibid.*, 4 December 1868.
35 *Ibid.*, January 1864.   36 *Ibid.*, January 1865.
37 *Ibid.*   38 *Ibid.*, May 1865.
39 *Ibid.*, October 1865.   40 *Ibid.*, 4 February 1869.
41 *Ibid.*, 20 March 1870.   42 *Ibid.*, 22 May 1870.
43 *Ibid.*, 20 April 1868.   44 *Ibid.*, 4 February 1869.
45 *Ibid.*, April 1866.   46 *Ibid.*, 4 February 1869.
47 *Ibid.*, 22 May, 1870.   48 *Ibid.*, 17 May 1867.
49 *Ibid.*   50 *Ibid.*, April 1870.

51 *Ibid.*, April 1866.

52 *Ibid.*, 12 August 1866.

53 *Ibid.*, May 1867.

54 *Ibid.*, November 1864.

55 *Ibid.*, 7 January 1869.

56 *Ibid.*, 14 November 1869.

57 *Ibid.*, 18 August 1868.

58 *Ibid.*

59 *Ibid.*, 5 December 1866.

60 *Ibid.*, February 1865.

61 *Ibid.*, 1864.

62 *Ibid.*, 31 December 1865.

63 *Ibid.*, July 1866.

64 *Ibid.*, 14 May 1867.

65 *Ibid.*, 17 May 1867.

66 *Ibid.*

67 *Ibid.*

68 *Ibid.*

69 *Igitur, Oeuvres Complètes*, Pléiade, 1945, p. 443.

70 *Correspondance*, 14 November 1869.

71 *Oeuvres Complètes*, p. 52.

72 *Correspondance*, 3 May 1868.

73 *Oeuvres Complètes* p. 273. 'Laments' translates '*sanglotte*', which, in view of the '*spasme de la glotte*' which was to kill Mallarmé, might be read as '*sans glotte*' (without a glottis).

74 *Ballets, Oeuvres Complètes*, p. 307.

75 *Correspondance*, 20 April 1868.

76 *Ibid.*, 23 August 1866.

77 *Ibid.*, 18 July 1868.

78 *Oeuvres Complètes*, p. 852.

79 *Ibid.*

80 *Ibid.*, 31 December 1869.

81 *Ibid.*, 20 March 1870.

82 *Ibid.*, April 1870.

83 *Oeuvres Complètes*, p. 258.

84 *Correspondance*, 29 April, 1870.

85 *Oeuvres Complètes*, p. 663.

86 *Ibid.*, p. 220.

87 Dr Soulier, *Lautréamont, génie ou maladie mentale?*, Minard, 1978; J. Fretet, *op. cit.*

88 J. Kristeva, *La Révolution du langage poétique*, Seuil, 1973.

89 The best being the one provided by François Caradec.

90 *Oeuvres Complètes*, p. 386.

91 *Ibid.*, pp. 1051–2.

92 Michel Foucault, *Les mots et les choses*, Gallimard, 1966, p. 298.

93 *Ibid.*

94 Mallarmé, *Oeuvres Complètes*, p. 920.

95 *Ibid.*, p. 855.

96 *Ibid.*, p. 919.

97 *Ibid.*, p. 921.

98 *Ibid.*, p. 926

99 *Ibid.*, p. 921.

100 Foucault, *op. cit.*, p. 300. The entire problematic of the relation between root and radical begins here. Cf. M. Foucault, *op. cit.*, Mallarmé, *Oeuvres Complètes*, p. 962; and J. Roudaut's discussion of the subject.

101 Mallarmé, *Oeuvres Complètes*, p. 852.

102 *Ibid.*, p. 903.

103 *Ibid.*, p. 139.

104 H. Mondor, *Vie de Mallarmé*, Gallimard, 1941, p. 412, note 1.

3 The power of Babel

* This title (*La Tour de Babil*) is borrowed from Wolfson's work. Fragments of

this chapter have appeared with the same title in *Recherches*, CERFI, 16, September 1974, and in *Semiotexte*, New York, vol. II, 1, 1975.

1 Photographic edition of the 1879 original, p. 1.
2 *Ibid.*, p. 602.
3 Cited in J. Starobinski, *Les mots sous les mots*, Gallimard, p. 20. Letter of 14 July 1906. According to the data provided by Jean Starobinski in his book, Saussure appears to have worked on the 'anagrams' from 1906 to 1909, and on the Germanic legends from 1903 to 1910 (and surely beyond); as for the 'Course in general linguistics', a review of J. Starobinski's book in *Cahiers Ferdinand de Saussure*, 27, 1971, pp. 123–5, notes that it only really started up in the second season of teaching, from November 1908 to January 1909. Therefore, there was a period in which Saussure, who was still searching for 'historical' proof of his discovery, had already shifted the organization of his linguistic conceptions to another stage. This epistemological ambiguity, sufficiently brief to have been but the crossing of a threshold, nevertheless would not be wholly removed until the anagrammatic theory had been definitively abandoned. And it is clearly as of this moment that *all* speculation on the origin of language and of languages acquires a different status: a new distribution of discourses is instituted between linguistics and psychiatry, which permits the modern classification of the different 'theories' on language, oscillating between 'science' and 'madness'. *After* Saussure, nothing that had been repeated or rediscovered of what Président de Brosses, Court de Gébelin or even Nodier had said (cf. G. Genette, J. Roudaut) could be read in the same way that it had been *before* Saussure. What could be science in the eighteenth century, then mere unreason in the nineteenth (that is, poetic theory as well), would have to choose between knowledge and madness:

> On the contrary, the nineteenth and twentieth centuries brought the entire weight of their interrogation to bear upon the analytical consciousness of madness; the other forms were but approximations, primitive attempts, archaic elements. And yet the Nietzschean critique, the values invested in separating the insane from the sane, and the great research which Artaud, following Nerval, mercilessly conducted upon himself, bear sufficient witness to the fact that all other forms of the awareness of madness still live at the heart of our culture. That they may now only be formulated in lyrical terms does not prove that they are vanishing, nor that they persist in prolonging an existence which knowledge has long since rejected, but that, maintained in the shadows, they flourish in the freest and most original forms of language. And their power to challenge is surely all the more vigorous. (M. Foucault, *Histoire de la folie à l'âge classique*, Gallimard, 1972, 2nd edn, p. 187.)

Relying upon a neighbouring analysis, we seek to show here that 'logophilia' remains, in our culture, the vital locus of the redistribution of these givens: operator of the metamorphoses of the episteme, of desire and of writing.

4 Starobinski, *op cit.*, p. 21. Saussure's italics. Furthermore, he rejoins Mallarmé here in a literal manner:

Through a superior and free instinct, it will devolve to the poet or
even to the scholarly prosator to bring together terms united all for
the better if they conform to the charm and to the music of language,
that they will reach us from all the more fortuitous distances: this
is the procedure inherent to the Northern genius, so many of whose
verses show us so many examples of alliteration. (Mallarmé, *Oeuvres
Complètes*, p. 921.)

Saussure does not appear to establish any privileged link between alliteration
and the North despite the studies on ancient Germanic legends, just as
Mallarmé neglects the presence of this phenomenon in Greek poetry. None
the less, in speaking of alliteration, Mallarmé confirms his logophilic relation
to the first Saussure, whereas his reference to the latter as a 'procedure'
brings him closer to Roussel, as we shall see.

5 Saussure, in Starobinski, *op. cit.*, p. 138.

6 R. Roussel, *Comment j'ai écrit certains de mes livres*, Roussel, 1935, p. 26.

7 Fr Caradec, *Vie de Raymond Roussel*, Pauvert, 1972, p. 36.

8 Roussel, *op. cit.*, p. 128.

9 *Ibid.*, p. 28.

10 L. Wolfson, *Le Schizo et les langues*, Gallimard, 1970.

11 *Ibid.*, p. 33.

12 *Ibid.*

13 Jean-Pierre Brisset, *La Grammaire logique*, with *La Science de Dieu*, Tchou,
   1970, p. 3.

14 *Ibid.*, p. 4.   15 *Ibid.*, p. 67.

16 *Ibid.*, p. 112.   17 *Ibid.*, p. 114.

18 *Ibid.*, p. 120.   19 *Ibid.*, p. 300.

20 *Ibid.*, p. 122.   21 *Ibid.*, p. 123.

22 *Ibid.*, p. 115.   23 *Ibid.*, p. 103.

24 Plato, *Cratyle*, Budé edn, p. 421.   25 Saussure, *op. cit.*, pp. 582–3.

26 *Ibid.*

27 Sylvain Auroux, *L'Encyclopédie: 'grammaire' et 'langue' au XVIIIe siècle*,
   Series Repères, Mame 1973, pp. 44, 46.

28 The symbol for infinity, or the classic image of a Moebius strip.

29 In 'Schizologie', introduction to Wolfson's book.

30 J. - P. Brisset, *op. cit.*, p. 175. Linguistics has certainly maintained close relations with organicism, the model for zoological organization. Cf. for example
   this sentence by Cuvier: 'All of the organs of a single animal form a unique
   system, all parts of which uphold each other, and act and react with each
   other: there can be no modification in one that does not bring about analo-
   gous changes in all the others.' *Rapport historique sur l'état des sciences
   naturelles*, cited in M. Foucault, *Les mots et les choses*, Gallimard, 1966,
   p. 277.

31 Brisset, *op. cit.*, p. 103.

32 Auroux, *op. cit.*, p. 17. See also Pierre Juliard, *Philosophies of Language in
   Eighteenth-Century France*, Mouton, 1970, Janua Linguarum, series minor,
   vol. 18, which offers a useful recapitulation of the different theories in existence. We have made use (*infra*) of some of his indications.

33 Brisset, *op. cit.*, p. 103.
34 G. Mounin, *Histoire de la linguistique*, P.U.F., 1967, p. 173.
35 Brisset, *op. cit.*, p. 67.
36 *Ibid.*, p. 74. Here we see the limits of the relations between logophilia and strict Cratylism, with Saussure hesitating between the two; whereas the entire thrust of Brisset's undertaking concentrates on the investigation of the origin, Socrates posits with precision a certain number of reference points that should not be lost from sight during the investigation of names: during his interpretation of Greek words, he only has exceptional recourse to explanations derived from other languages and, when doing so, never follows through. Inversely, he makes it a rule never to 'try to demonstrate the correctness of foreign names in reference to the Hellenic language'. Strict monoglossia: the language is always limited by an exterior which preserves it from adventures by assigning it an identity. In the same way, Socrates recognizes that there are primary, indivisible words; in other words, the system does not give way to a regression *ad infinitum* which would truly call into question the meaning of the origin, as it would the origin of meaning. Such an origin remains inaccessible to it, and this function of inaccessibility is guaranteed by the gods themselves, who are, by definition, unknowable. There is a need here to examine the relations between such a conception of the signifier and the seemingly isomorphous conception of numbers: the existence of numbers and of 'primary' names; the status of the signifier as a positive rationale; the relations between a zero and an origin, etc. Daniel Sibony's *Le nom et le corps* (especially: 'L'infini et la castration') contains an investigation which is not without relations to this one.
   In the case of Saussure, it is the production of the notion of *system* which permits doing away with the question (phantasmatic and menacing) of the origin. In this manner, he saves his reason, *the* linguistic reason, by producing the theoretical means which definitively permit the *subject* to be detached from the language. Cf. '*The principle of the subordination of signification to value can, in our estimation, be considered as the core of the Saussurian rupture.* It is this principle, closely tied to the idea of the language as system, which opens the possibility for a general theory of the language which permits the interpretation of the phonological, syntactic and morphological particularities of any given language. But what of semantics? As a result of the role attributed there to speech and to the subject, everything which concerns the analogy is pre-empted by this rupture, for the subordination of signification to value for everything which concerns 'the linguistic fact in its essence and amplitude' has precisely the effect of cutting short any return to the subject, when it is a question of the language: signification is on the order of speech and of the subject, value alone concerns the language.' Cf. Haroche, P. Henry and M. Pecheux: 'La sémantique et la coupure saussurienne: langue, langage, discours', in *Langages*, 24, Larousse, 1976.
37 Brisset, *op. cit.*, 185.
38 *Ibid.* p. 104.
39 *Ibid.* My italics.
40 This is the study of the *Memoirs of a neuropath* by Président Schreber; *Gesammelte Werke*, vol. VIII, *Standard Edition*, vol. XII. For a different

point of view on this *princeps* case, cf. Morton Schatzman, *Soul Murders*.

41 F. de Saussure, *Recueil des Publications Scientifiques*, Geneva, 1922, Slatkine Reprint, Geneva, 1970, p. 19. My italics.

42 *Ibid.*

43 *Ibid.*, p. 21.

44 *Ibid.*, p. 602.

45 Brisset, *op. cit.*, p. 146. The italics are his own. We could say of Brisset, as of all his logophilic predecessors, that he makes units of secondary articulation (Martinet) from signifying elements. It is therefore as of this moment that languages (the Word) signify, according to him, and not when these elements combine to form 'monemes', that is, lexicalized signs. Whence, given the relative poverty of the possible phonological choices, the *necessary* practice of 'panglossia'.

46 *Ibid.*

47 *Ibid.*, p. 147.

48 *Ibid.*, p. 148.

49 L. Wolfson, *Le Schizo et les langues*, Gallimard, 1970, p. 33. Wolfson's experience must still be understood against the more general backdrop of the relations which the schizophrenic is said to maintain with language. It seems that the differences are important, since

> the schizophrenic who lacks this reciprocal exchange between the mirror and his "body" is the signifier's plaything. His discourse evokes a new language, made up entirely of substitutions, of neoforms which he wishes equivalent, pseudo-metaphors because they do not actually have a cipher. Here, the axis of contiguity collapses. A fireworks display, his discourse fascinates with the freedom of its creation, its playful matter-of-factness. Its lack of meaning, however, can be detected in the fading of intonation and of articulation, as in those moments when the "subject", listening, waits for language itself to take up his play, for which he is the spokesman and not really the speaker. The language, having become the free activity of generations and transformations, would take the place of the subject of the speech act (L. Irigaray, 'Communications linguistique et spéculaire', in *Cahiers pour l'analyse*, 3, 1966, p. 53).

Wolfson's position before language does seem to derive from a logic which responds to other rules.

50 *Ibid.*, p. 33.

51 Saussure, in Starobinski *op. cit.*, p. 125. The italics are his own. Here he reaches the most extreme limit which he could, 'reasonably' or 'unreasonably', attain, but not go beyond, lest he plummet into an entirely different universe, for, as Roman Jakobson recalls, 'The poetic anagram crosses over the two "fundamental laws of the human word" proclaimed by Saussure, that of the codified bond between a signifier and its signified, and that of the linearity of the signifiers.' In 'La première lettre de Ferdinand de Saussure à Antoine Meillet sur les annagrammes', letter published and commented upon by R. Jakobson in *L'Homme*. 11, 1971, p. 23. Fr Rastier, furthermore,

confirms the phantasmatic nature of Saussure's quest, including even from a strictly philological point of view – which is after all the starting point for this quest – when she writes: 'We call "Saturnian" those verses which do not enter into the frame of classical metrics . . .', or when she concludes: 'In the absence of a preliminary definition of the 'Saturnian,' we do not know where to address a verification of Saussure's theories, *that is, we have no way of stating what is their object.*' In 'A propos du Saturnien', *Latomus*, XXIX, fasc. 1, 1970. My italics.

52 Roussel, *op. cit.*, p. 11.
53 *Ibid.*, p. 13.
54 *Ibid.*, p. 20.

4 Figuration of a delirium: Brisset and the 'Science of God'

* This chapter resumes and develops certain analyses which appeared under the title: 'The adventures of the Lord God and the Unwed-Mother', in *Le Siècle éclaté*, 1, Minard, 1974.

1 Brisset must evidently be classified among the typical cases of paranoia; we shall endeavour to show this in reference to Freud's classical study, even though our object here does not concern the analysis of a psychosis as such.

2 Cf. n. 19, Ch. 3.

3 Brisset, *Grammaire Logique*, Tchou, 1970, p. 112. Let us recall that hallucination appears as 'the aesthetic *and* libidinal mode appropriate to psychosis, in the unparalleled tension of a hallucinatory-living, the inexhaustible echo of the desiring-living which is the founding structure of the so-called normal or neurotic subject.' 'Introduction critique à l'étude de l'hallucination', *Scilicet*, 1, Seuil, 1968, p. 120.

4 *Ibid.*, p. 11.

5 *Ibid.*, p. 161.

6 *Ibid.*, p. 158. The analysis cited hereunder (cf. note 3) also permits accounting for the signifier which takes shape behind each word in the course of Brisset's investigation – the desired and menacing phallus –

> the hallucinatory object primordially and in its essence concerns the genital sphere; there is no clinical example of its not playing the primary role in the delirium; this is true to such an extent that it is possible to posit that every hallucination, whatever its localization or mode of expression, is by nature genital. The hallucinatory Voice appears here as a partial object, in an equivalence which concerns the sexual organ. (*Scilicet*, p. 133.)

This is also confirmed by Serge Leclaire when he writes: 'It seems to us that the *psychotic organization*, unlike 'normal' or neurotic organizations, is characterized by the *lack of an assured split, or articulation, between the literal space and the body*. The letter never stops turning back upon the body, and nothing then permits distinguishing the body from words.' 'Les mots du psychotique', in *Change*, 12, 1972. Brisset would therefore be staging a relatively displaced version of this process, since he retains the ability to represent it as a representation.

In seeking throughout all languages to rediscover the discourse of the voice heard on the banks of the frog pond, Brisset does in fact behave like that hallucinator who, according to the study cited above (cf. note 3),

> undertakes to desperately seek out that subject who has now become
> a sender, and whom he never succeeds, and for good reason, in
> tracking down . . . , witnesses to that translation which causes him
> to misrecognize his own being in the organizer, the subject of the
> Voice, the one that warns his own unrecognized thoughts to turn
> around, and whose phonemes his larynx involuntarily and silently
> articulates. (*Scilicet*, p. 134.)

Instead of recognizing the inflexion of his own voice in what the Word says, Brisset will settle into it entirely, and become the pure instrument of its articulation.

On the question of the phantasy in general, and on its link to speech and the look, cf. C. Backès-Clément, 'De la méconnaissance: Fantasme, texte, scène', in *Langages*, 31.

7 Brisset, *op. cit.*, p. 292.

8 *Ibid.*, p. 246.
9 *Ibid.*, p. 328.
10 *Ibid.*, p. 316.
11 *Ibid.*, p. 248.
12 *Ibid.*, p. 253.
13 *Ibid.*, p. 305.
14 *Ibid.*, p. 218.
15 *Ibid.*, p. 307.
16 *Ibid.*, p. 310.
17 *Ibid.*, p. 180.
18 *Ibid.*, p. 117.
19 *Ibid.*, p. 146.
20 *Ibid.*, p. 147.
21 *Ibid.*, p. 171.
22 *Ibid.*, p. 170.
23 *Ibid.*, p. 180.
24 *Ibid.*, p. 181.
25 *Ibid.*, p. 246.
26 *Ibid.*, p. 271.
27 *Ibid.*, p. 150.
28 *Ibid.*, p. 310.
29 *Ibid.*, p. 320.
30 *Ibid.*, p. 321.
31 *Ibid.*, p. 253.
32 *Ibid.*, p. 181.
33 *Ibid.*
34 *Ibid.*, p. 254.
35 *Ibid.*, p. 316.
36 *Ibid.*, p. 181.
37 *Ibid.*, p. 212.
38 *Ibid.*, p. 87.
39 *Ibid.*, p. 192.
40 *Ibid.*, p. 188.
41 *Ibid.*, p. 189.
42 *Ibid.*, p. 189.
43 *Ibid.*, p. 188.
44 *Ibid.*
45 *Ibid.*, p. 290.
46 *Ibid.*, p. 189.
47 *Ibid.*, p. 296.
48 *Ibid.*, p. 251.
49 *Ibid.*, cf. note 40.
50 *Ibid.*, p. 246.
51 *Ibid.*, p. 288.
52 *Ibid.*
53 *Ibid.*, p. 244.
54 *Ibid.*, p. 316.

Conclusion

1 Saussure, in Starobinski, *Les mots sous les mots*, Gallimard, p. 132.
2 Roussel, *Comment j'ai écrit certains de mes livres*, Roussel, 1935.
3 Brisset, *Grammaire Logique*, Tchou, 1970, p. 327.
4   For – and this may be one of the fundamental traits of our culture –
    it is not possible to maintain oneself in a decisive and infinitely
    resolute manner in this distance of unreason. It must be forgotten
    and abolished, as soon as it is measured in the vertigo of the sen-
    sible and the reclusion of madness. (M. Foucault, *Histoire de la
    folie à l'âge classique*, Gallimard, 1972, p. 371.)

Index

As references to Mallarmé, Saussure, Roussel, Brisset, and Wolfson appear on virtually every page of this volume, only those pages in which there are sustained discussions of these authors are noted.